POLISH WINGS 39

Bartłomiej Belcarz
Franciszek Strzelczyk

Caudron-Renault CR.714 Cyclone

STRATUS

Wydawnictwo STRATUS sp.j.
ul. Żeromskiego 6A, 27-600 Sandomierz, Poland
e-mail: office@stratusbooks.pl
www.stratusbooks.com.pl www.mmpbooks.biz

ISBN 978-83-67227-58-2

Layout concept	*the late Bartłomiej Belcarz*
Cover concept	*Artur Juszczak*
Cover	*Marek Ryś*
Layout	*the late Bartłomiej Belcarz*
DTP	*Stratus sp.j.*
Text	*the late Bartłomiej Belcarz, Franciszek Strzelczyk*
Text editing and translation	*Wojtek Matusiak*
Proofreading	*Roger Wallsgrowe*
Colour plates	*Karolina Hołda, Artur Juszczak*
Photo-map diagrams	*Thierry Vallet*

PRINTED IN POLAND

Photographs from the following persons and institutions have been used in the publication: the late Bartłomiej Belcarz, Mathieu Comas, Philippe Couderchon, James Crow, Jarosław Dobrzyński, J.M. Goyat, Robert Gretzyngier, Zbigniew Lalak, Thomas Rajkowski, Philippe Ricco, Peter Sikora, Paweł Tuliński, Grzegorz Zaleski; Polish Aviation Museum (Cracow), Finnish Air Force Museum, Polish Institute & Sikorski Museum (London), SHD (Paris).

Bartek Belcarz

He was a man of Renaissance nature. A history teacher who imparted his knowledge to his students at a high school in Stalowa Wola in a unique, engaging manner, a tutor to uniformed classes, a passionate explorer of unknown aspects of Polish history, a modeller, and the organiser of famous modelling festivals in Stalowa Wola, which attracted enthusiasts from both Poland and abroad. But above all, he was an author and researcher, who popularised in his countless books and articles what excited him most: the unknown chapters of Polish aviation history during the 1940 French campaign. He was also a well-known and respected publisher – a co-founder of the Stratus publishing house, whose reputation and the highest level of English-language books are renowned in the entire aviation-minded world. His activity also included events organised in France, to remind the people there of the few Poles who fought, triumphed, and perished in her skies. He organised exhibitions, lectures, and talks, which made many people realise that the Poles not only made a significant contribution to the defence of London against the *Luftwaffe*, but also to that of Paris.

His family: his wife, daughter, two sons, and grandchildren, undoubtedly provided support and inspiration for him. The moments he shared with his loved ones reflected his rich private life, as full of love and dedication as his professional one.

He worked with immense dedication, facing physical ailments bravely until the end. His publications released in late 2023 and early 2024 are a testimony to that.

We deeply and painfully mourn his passing. For he was a unique man, full of inner warmth and kindness. We will miss him very, very much. There can be no illusion: a gap has been created in the community of researchers of Polish aviation history that will no longer be filled with his invaluable knowledge. There will no longer be that great passion for discovering everything related to the Poles in air force uniforms thrown by a caprice of fate onto French territories in 1940.

The CR.714 with the Polish Air Force

Lyon

The first Caudron-Renault CR.714s were delivered to the DIAP (CWL) at Lyon on 10 March 1940.

The CR.714 deliveries were connected with the decision to form a special fighter squadron, known as the 'Finland Squadron', from Polish personnel, which would be used against the USSR during the Winter War. Recruitment to the unit was on a voluntary basis among pilots who were at the BA 145 (Base Aérienne No. 145) at Lyon-Bron. About 150 pilots applied, five times more than the establishment number in the squadron.

In March 1940, only the pilots planned to be sent to Finland were flying the Caudrons at Lyon. It is difficult to determine exactly how many aircraft of the type were at the base at the time.

Two unidentified CR.714s were photographed on 27 March 1940, when the farewell ceremony of the 'Montpellier Escadrille' took place in Lyon.

Unfortunately, essentially only two flying log books of GC 1/145 pilots are known. Based on the entries in these (and in flying log books of other pilots based in Lyon at the time) and on memoirs it can be ascertained that in early March 1940 the CR.714s were used only by pilots of the 'Finland Squadron'[1].

It can also hardly be considered as training on the type. Usually the pilots simply flew several introductory flights in order to get familiarised with the specific characteristics of the aeroplane rather than completing any training program syllabus.

1 The 'Finland Squadron' was the forerunner of the GC 1/145.

*[1]: On 27 March the Lyon-Bron airfield saw the largest ceremony in the history of the exiled Polish Air Force in France in 1940: a solemn farewell to the first group of pilots posted for attachment to French units. The troops assembled in the parade ground await the arrival of Gen. Sikorski and other guests. The Ceremonial Company of the DIAP is standing with their backs to the camera. Facing them, on the left, are officers of the DIAP who formed five company (*Escadrille*) troops during the ceremony, the DIAP HQ and the fighter pilots of French front-line units who arrived for the ceremony. (MLP)*

1

[2]: *Gen. Władysław Sikorski talking to Gen. Denain. Col. Hug, the French commander of the DIAP Lyon, and Gen. Józef Zając, commanding the Polish Air Force, are listening to the conversation. (PI&SM)*

Directing the pilots of the 'Finland Squadron' to get familiarised with CR.714 was a logical step. Following the 'Montpellier Escadrille', it was the second group of Polish pilots intended for extensive training. In March, the final decision to equip the emerging squadron with the CR.714 had not been taken yet, and probably that was why further training continued on the Morane Saulnier MS.406s. In addition, as mentioned earlier, there were not enough CR.714s at the BA 145 to provide adequate training for the entire unit then being formed.

The first problems with the Caudrons occurred immediately after the training began. The first aircraft was damaged on 13 March 1940, three days after the flying started. Due to incorrect handling of the propeller pitch control mechanism, the engine overheated and it was damaged after 25 minutes of flight. The aeroplane, flown by 2nd Lt Eugeniusz Fiedorczuk, was forced to land. The engine was beyond repair. No information is available about any injuries to the pilot. The aircraft, c/n 8547 (I-205, white 3), was sent away for repairs. The aircraft was then captured by the Germans in June 1940 at the Lyon-Bron airfield (after the engine was replaced).

Further problems occurred during the training flight of Lt Witold Łanowski on 15 March 1940. About 11.15 CR.714 c/n 8548 (I-205, white 4?) was coming in to land. The pilot had technical problems with the lowering of the undercarriage. During repeated attempts only one main wheel leg would lower. For about 40 minutes the pilot tried to force the undercarriage down by various manoeuvres, but without success. When the aeroplane began to run out of fuel, he decided to land on the one wheel. Luckily for Łanowski, at the first impact of the wheel on the surface of the airfield, the other leg dropped and the pilot landed safely. The aircraft was handed over for an inspection of the undercarriage system.

Other pilots who were training in Lyon also started flying the CR.714 at the beginning of April immediately after Sikorski's visit. The crash of LtWitold Dobrzyński (probably in c/n 8548, I-206) was one of two tragic accidents involving the CR.714 in Lyon. On 19 April 1940, his aeroplane stalled when coming in to land, due to lack of speed.

The accident made quite a big impression on the staff in Lyon, because it happened in front of many witnesses. Dobrzyński died in the ambulance on the way to the Sick Quarters. His body was taken to the Desgenettes military hospital. The accident was described by Lt Mirosław Ferić in his diary: "Lt Dobrzyński Witold is killed during training on

3

[3]: The march past of the Ceremonial Company, led by Capt. Edmund Jura, during the ceremony at Lyon-Bron on 27 March 1940. (MLP)

the Cyclones, nicknamed 'Strzałki' ('Darts')[2] by the late Czesio Sałkiewicz[3]. While returning from aerobatics, during a normal circuit of the airfield, the round to the port before landing, his prop started to stop due to lack of fuel, the machine went down suddenly without responding to the controls, because with its small wing area and no altitude there was no way it would reach the airfield. The machine hit the ditch next to the asphalt road with its engine, this being the most tragic moment for the pilot, jumped up, bounced, and fell a few meters away."[4]

There was more trouble with the CR.714 on 17 May 1940, when the GC 1/145 was preparing to leave for the front line. About 14.15 Cpl Marian Wędzik, a GC 1/145 pilot, forced landed near Villars-les-Dombes (25 km north-east of Lyon) in c/n 8581 (I-239). The aeroplane had flown relatively little, a total of 2 hrs 55 min. (the accumulated flying time of the engine had been 3 hrs 15 min.). The propeller and the star board tailplane were damaged in the landing. The next day the aeroplane was salvaged and taken to Parc 5/102 (repair workshops). In June 1940, this machine was captured by the Germans when they occupied the base at Lyon.

Despite the lack of access to many flying log books, existing data allowed compiling the following list of machines used at DIAP Lyon.

Numbers of the CR.714s at the Lyon Bron air base in 1940

Military serial no.	Under-wing no. (*Matricule Militaire*)	Construction no.	Code no.	Notes
8	I-198	8540		GC 1/145
12	I-202	8544		GC 1/145
13	I-203	8545	1	Clermont-Ferrand
14	I-204	8546	2	Kornicki
15	I-205	8547	3	
16	I-206	8548	4?	Dobrzyński
26	I-216	8558	5?	
27	I-217	8559	6	
28	I-218	8560	7	Schmidt
29	I-219	8561		
42	I-232	8574		
44	I-234	8576		GC 1/145
49	I-239	8581		Wędzik
51	I-241	8583		GC 1/145

The first Caudron-Renault CR.714s were taken on charge by the GC 1/145 from the factory as late as 17 May 1940.[5]

The remaining Caudrons were still used at the DIAP to train subsequent fighter pilots. Similar to the GC 1/145 pilots, as a rule, each pilot completed several familiarisation flights in

2 An interesting comment about an unofficial name of the CR.714 used among Polish pilots at Lyon.

3 Lt Czesław Sałkiewicz, commanding the DAT section at Toulouse. He was killed in a flying accident on 30 May 1940 at 20.10 in Dewoitine D 520 c/n 99 when coming in to land upon return from a patrol.

4 M. Ferić, *Pamiętnik pilota...*, PI&SM London, LOT A V 49/34/2.

5 The group that collected the CR.714s included 2nd Lt Stanisław Łukaszewicz.

[4]: The ceremony at the DIAP Lyon-Bron on 27 March 1940. The Officers' Assembly Pool and the 'Montpellier Escadrille' staff march in front of the invited guests. DIAP aeroplanes can be seen in the background. Left to right: a Morane Saulnier MS.406, a Caudron-Renault CR.714 and a Potez 63-11. (MLP)

[5]: Lt Witold Dobrzyński (1913–1940) was the first fatal casualty of the training on Caudron-Renault CR.714s. His aeroplane, c/n 8548 (I-206), crashed at the edge of the airfield at Bron on 19 April 1940.

[6]: His funeral on 22 April 1940: the funeral procession at the Guillotière cemetery.

[7]: 2nd Lt Jan Daszewski (3rd left), 2nd Lt Czesław Główczyński (4th), 2nd Lt Bolesław Gładych (5th), Lt Wojciech Januszewicz, salute his grave. (PI&SM)

8

9

[8–11]: A hangar at Lyon-Bron with CR.714 c/n 8547 (I-205). Note old style small size roundels on the wing upper surface. The photos were taken after the Germans occupied the Lyon-Bron airfield. ([8–10] B. Belcarz coll. [11] Z.Lalak coll.)

10

11

the total time of several dozen minutes, after which he moved on to the next type, the Morane Saulnier MS.406.

After the German attack, fighter sections were formed from the Training Fighter Flight in Lyon to defend the city and the base. The sections were equipped with the Morane Saulnier MS.406s. The nine remaining Caudrons were used only for fighter training. From the time of the German assault, this was conducted at the satellite airfield at Mions (St Symphorien d'Ozon). The departure of the GC 1/145 did not change the training syllabus.

Unfortunately, more casualties were not avoided. CR.714 c/n 8560 (I-218) was another aeroplane struck off charge of the DIAP, destroyed in a collision with Caudron C.635 c/n 295[6]. The accident, in which 2nd Lt Stanisław Kogut, the pilot of the C.635 was killed, was caused by the CR.714's pilot, 2nd Lt Jerzy Schmidt. The crash took place on 5 June 1940 at 9.20 a.m. at the Mions airfield. The C.635 flown by 2nd Lt Kogut (with 2nd Lt Zygmunt Drybański as passenger) landed during flying training and waited for a signal to taxi. The CR.714 of 2nd Lt Jerzy Schmidt prepared to take off at that same time. During the take-off run it swung to the starboard and hit the C.635 with great force. 2nd Lt Stanisław Kogut was killed, the others were injured, and both aeroplanes caught fire.

The rapid progress of German troops has put the Lyon airfield in danger. DIAP staff was evacuated, the aeroplanes were left at the airfield. After Lyon was occupied by the Germans, they also captured the aeroplanes at the airfield. At least five CR.714s had remained in Lyon. This is confirmed by the report prepared at the Lyon-Bron base on 16 August 1940, in which the following machines were listed:

Military serial no.	Under-wing no. (*Matricule Militaire*)	Construction no.	Code no.	Notes
15	I-205	8547	3	
27	I-217	8559	6	
29	I-219	8561		
42	I-232	8574		
49	I-239	8581		GC 1/145

The list includes, among others, c/n 8574 (I-232) which did not appear in any of the pilot's flying log books of either the GC 1/145 or the DIAP Lyon-Bron. It was probably a replacement delivered to DIAP at Base Aérienne No. 145 Lyon-Bron in the first half of May 1940.

Probably three Caudron-Renault CR.714s left Lyon during the evacuation. One of these, c/n 8545 (I-203), was destroyed at Clermont-Ferrand just after the Germans entered, in an act of pure vandalism. The scenes of its destruction were included in a German newsreel, in which the commentator identified Clermont-Ferrand as the place where the scenes were shot.

12

[12]: Caudron-Renault CR.714 c/n 8547, serial no. 15, code no. 3 (under-wing no. I-205). Fighter Training Flight, DIAP, Lyon-Bron, May 1940.

6 Various documents related to the accident quote the construction number as either 293 or 295.

Known photos of the remains of a burnt-out wreck of a CR.714 at the airfield additionally confirm the presence of the type at Clermont. It is yet to be clarified whether it was the CR.714 mentioned above, c/n 8545 (I-203), or perhaps one of two other aircraft of the type, c/ns 8546 (I-204) and 8558 (I-216), the fate of which remains unknown. Perhaps they shared the same fate as c/n 8545 (I-203)?

[13, 14]: Cad. Off. Sołogub by a Curtiss Hawk H-75 of the GC II/5. The photo was taken at Mions on 16 June 1940. CR.714 no. 13, I-203, white 1, can be seen in the background. (B. Belcarz coll. & P. Sikora coll.)

[15]: A frame from a German propaganda film showing the destruction of CR.714 serial no. 13 (I-203) at Clermont-Ferrand-Aulnat. (J.M. Goyat coll.)

[16]: Clermont-Ferrand. The burnt-out engine section in the foreground is most probably from CR.714 serial no. 13 (I-203). The MS.406 behind it is c/n 875, code no. 6, evacuated from Avord. (B. Belcarz coll.)

17

18

[17–20]: Caudron-Renault CR.714 c/n 8559, serial no. 27, code no. 6 (under-wing no. I-217). Fighter Training Flight, DIAP, Lyon-Bron, June 1940.

19

20

[21–24]: Caudron-Renault CR.714 c/n 8559 (serial no. 27, I-217, code no. 6) inside and in front of the Lyon-Bron hangar in June 1940. Initially, the aeroplane together with CR.714 c/n 8547 (serial no. 15, I-205) was inside the hangar. (B. Belcarz coll. & G. Zaleski coll.)

[25, 26]: *Caudron-Renault CR.714 code no. 6 (I-217). After the Germans rolled it outside the hangar, the next stage was to set it up as if it was an aeroplane destroyed during operations. The most popular photo depicted it popped up onto its nose, which has revealed details of the disruptive camouflage on the wings. (B. Belcarz coll.)*

27

[27, 28]: German soldiers posing on a captured CR.714. Its identity (c/n 8581) could be identified thanks to the military serial number 49 on the pilot's headrest and the partly visible digits of the under-wing number (I-239). This aeroplane had to forceland near Lyon while ferried to the GC 1/145 on 17 May, damaging the propeller and the starboard tailplane. The unfortunate pilot, Cpl Marian Wędzik, was not injured, but he was not included in the GC 1/145 staff that left for Villacoublay the following day. (B. Belcarz coll.)

28

[29, 30]: *Caudron-Renault CR.714 c/n 8546, serial no. 14, code no. 2 (under-wing no. I-204). Fighter Training Flight, DIAP, Lyon-Mions, May 1940.*

29

30

31

[31]: Franciszek Kornicki, who was training at the Mions airfield, wrote in his memoirs of: "One day, shortly after take-off, I had an engine failure and decided to turn back to the airfield as there were woods on three sides. I managed, but only just, having to jump over some small trees on the edge of the airfield, which caused loss of speed and consequently I landed heavily; and bent the undercarriage and propeller quite a lot. As I was getting out of the wreck in disgust, and without a scratch, Captain Rougevin was speeding in my direction with his interpreter. He was not very happy with my explanations and thought I should have done better". A photo of the 'white 2' was published in Kornicki's book with an appropriate caption. (B. Belcarz & A. Zipser coll.)

32

[32, 33]: *No documents related to the accident of CR.714 c/n 8546 (I-204) are known. It took place at Mions (St Symphorien d'Ozon) airfield and the Caudron belonged to the DIAP Lyon. That was the period when the training of Polish pilots was transferred to Mions after the bombing of Bron. It was probably left there after the armistice, because it cannot be found in the list of aircraft captured by the Germans at the Bron base. (B. Belcarz & A. Zipser coll.)*

33

[34]: DIAP mechanics during a meal at Mions. Early June 1940. (B. Belcarz & A. Zipser coll.)

34

[35, 36]: The next aeroplane struck off charge by the DIAP was c/n 8560 (I-218) destroyed in a collision with Caudron C.635 c/n 295. The accident took place at 9:20 a.m. on 5 June 1940 at the Mions airfield. During flying training the C.635 flown by 2nd Lt Stanisław Kogut (with 2nd Lt Zygmunt Drybański as passenger) landed and waited for a signal for further taxiing. At the same time, the CR.714 with 2nd Lt Jerzy Schmidt at the controls prepared for takeoff. When he started his take-off, the aircraft swung to the starboard and hit the C.635 with great force. 2nd Lt Stanisław Kogut was killed, the others were wounded, and both aeroplanes caught fire. Photo [36] shows the Mions airfield with the burning aeroplanes in the background and ground crew members going to the scene of the accident. Photo [35] shows an unidentified Morane MS.406 of the DIAP, and behind it the destroyed CR.714 c/n 8560 (code no. 7, I-218). The picture is not very sharp, but clear enough to see the extensive damage to the nose of the Caudron. (B. Belcarz & A. Zipser coll.)

35

36

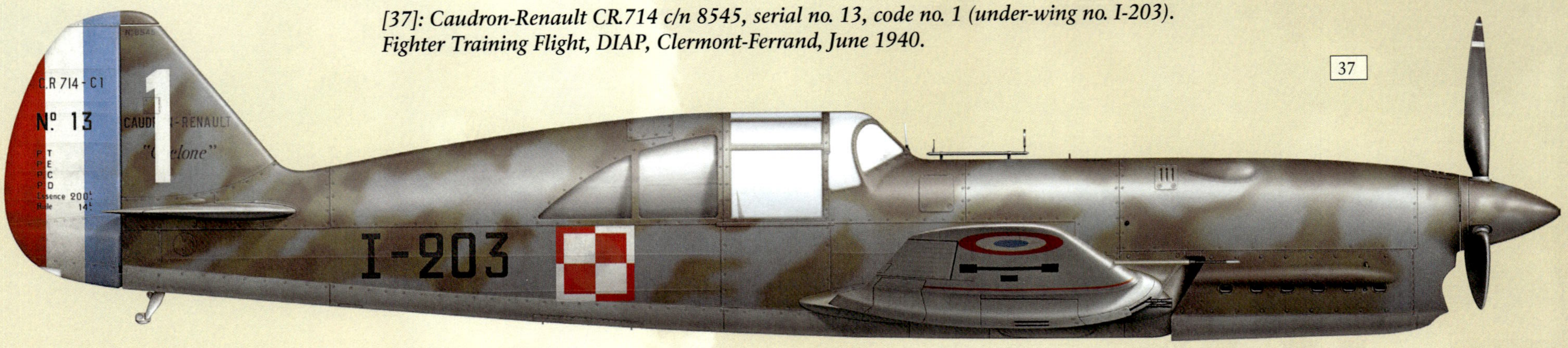

37

[37]: *Caudron-Renault CR.714 c/n 8545, serial no. 13, code no. 1 (under-wing no. I-203). Fighter Training Flight, DIAP, Clermont-Ferrand, June 1940.*

38

[38]: *CR.714 code no. 1 (I-203) was probably the only one of the type evacuated from Mions to Clermont-Ferrand. This is the only photograph of this machine that is clear enough to read the numbers of the aeroplane without a doubt. The photo was taken shortly before its destruction. Three chimneys of the Michelin factory at Clermont-Ferrand can be seen in the background on the left. (B. Belcarz & A. Zipser coll.)*

Short history of the GC 1/145

The Polish fighter squadron GC 1/145 'Varsovie' was the only operational unit that used the Caudron-Renault CR.714 in combat. The short but rather complicated history of the forming of this unit is outlined here.

Polish pilots who came to France were sent to various assembly stations, and the largest and most important of these, from the Polish viewpoint, was based at Lyon-Bron. It became the principal place of Polish personnel registration and the location where the first Polish air units were formed.

At the end of December 1939, the Polish fighter pilots in the base were (unofficially) split for the first time into separate groups that would form the basis for future fighter units.

Forming of two fighter and one observation squadrons was considered. However, rumours about the anticipated use

39

[39]: GC 1/145 personnel. A souvenir photo taken inside a hangar at Lyon-Bron. In the first row, left to right: Capt. Juliusz Frey, unknown, Capt. Antoni Wczelik, Cne Pierre Rougevin-Baville, Maj. Józef Kępiński, unknown, unknown, unknown, Capt. Mieczysław Wiórkiewicz. In the second row, left to right: unknown, unknown, unknown, Capt. Franciszek Fugiel, LAC Edward Uchto, Cpl Marian Wędzik, 2nd Lt Witold Łanowski, Lt Robert Janota, 2nd Lt Czesław Główczyński, Lt Tadeusz Czerwiński, Lt Jan Obuchowski, 2nd Lt Bronisław Skibiński, 2nd Lt Marian Łukaszewicz, Cpl Lucjan Szempliński, Lt Wacław Wilczewski, Cpl Edward Paterek, Capt. Piotr Łaguna, Lt Julian Kowalski, unknown, Capt. Józef Grzebalski, unknown. In the third row, left to right: 2nd Lt Lech Lachowicki-Czechowicz, Lt Zdzisław Zadroziński, 2nd Lt Bolesław Gładych, 2nd Lt Marian Szalewicz, LAC Jerzy Zieliński, Cpl Andrzej Niewiara, LAC Ernest Watolski, 2nd Lt Aleksy Żukowski, Cpl Jan Palak, LAC Piotr Zaniewski, Cpl Antoni Markiewicz, unknown, Lt Jerzy Godlewski, Cpl Antoni Siudak, 2nd Lt Leon Jaugsch, unknown. (PI&SM coll.)

Organisational structure of the Polish air units formed at DIAP Lyon in the spring of 1940.

CWL/DIAP Lyon-Bron

- **1st Fighter Squadron** – Commander Lt Col. Leopold Pamuła
  - Engineer Officer – Lt Konstanty Rydzewski
  - Liaison Officer – Maj. Eugeniusz Wyrwicki
  - 1st Flight Commander – Capt. Zdzislaw Krasnodębski
  - 2nd Flight Commander – Capt. Adam Kowalczyk
- **2nd Fighter Squadron** – Commander from 1 March 1940 Maj. Mieczysław Mümler
  - Engineer Officer – Capt. Franciszek Gomuliński
  - Liaison Officer – Capt. Mieczysław Sulerzycki
  - 1st Flight Commander – Capt. Franciszek Jastrzębski
  - 2nd Flight Commander – Capt. Stefan Łaszkiewicz
- **Observation Squadron** – Commander Maj. Edward Młynarski
  - Engineer Officer – Lt Adam Osuch
  - 1st Flight Commander – Capt. Czesław Kujawa
  - 2nd Flight Commander – Capt. Aleksander Łukiński

[40]: Bird's eye view of the Lyon-Bron airfield, spring 1940. The parking apron and civil airport hangars can be seen in the bottom of the photograph. (SHD coll.)

[41]: GC 1/145 personnel. A souvenir photo taken inside a hangar at Lyon-Bron. In the first row, left to right: Capt. Juliusz Frey, Capt. Franciszek Fugiel, Capt. Antoni Wczelik, Cne Pierre Rougevin-Baville, Maj. Józef Kępiński, Capt. Piotr Łaguna, Capt. Józef Grzebalski, Lt Julian Kowalski. In the second row, left to right: unknown, LAC Edward Uchto, Cpl Marian Wędzik, 2nd Lt Witold Łanowski, Lt Robert Janota, 2nd Lt Czesław Główczyński, Lt Tadeusz Czerwiński, Lt Jan Obuchowski, 2nd Lt Bronisław Skibiński, 2nd Lt Marian Łukaszewicz, Cpl Lucjan Szempliński, Lt Wacław Wilczewski, 2nd Lt Leon Jaugsch, Cpl Edward Paterek. In the third row, left to right: 2nd Lt Lech Lachowicki-Czechowicz, Lt Zdzisław Zadroziński, 2nd Lt Bolesław Gładych, 2nd Lt Marian Szalewicz, LAC Jerzy Zieliński, Cpl Andrzej Niewiara, LAC Ernest Watolski, 2nd Lt Aleksy Żukowski, LAC Piotr Zaniewski, Cpl Jan Palak, Cpl Antoni Markiewicz, Lt Jerzy Godlewski, Cpl Antoni Siudak. (PI&SM London coll.)

of a Polish expeditionary force (within Allied forces) to take part in the fighting of the Finns against the Russians led in January 1940 to announcement of voluntary recruitment among the personnel at Lyon Bron. The effects exceeded all expectations. Over 150 volunteers applied, of whom 61 officers and NCOs were selected, and placed under command of Maj. Józef Kępiński.

The first concept was to use the equipment provided by the British to Finland (a promise of the British Military Attaché in Sweden). However, the eventual decision was to form a two-*escadrille* (two-flight) fighter groupe (squadron) to fight in Finland as a unit of the Polish Air Force, reporting tactically to the Finnish HQ. The personnel would be trained in France and then transferred to Finland with the equipment.

The truce between the fighting countries resulted in a change of plans for the unit of Maj. Kępiński.[1] On 15 March 1940, Gen. Zając sent the following signal to the Commandant of the DIAP at Lyon Bron. "In connection with the conclusion of peace by Finland with Russia, I order that the current staff of the fighter sqn be replenished up to a full establishment of a fighter sqn intended for Finland as the III fighter squadron."[2]

Thus, on 15 March 1940, the group of Maj. Kępiński was officially called the III Fighter Squadron for the first time. A few days earlier that group of pilots had stared training on the Caudrons that had reached the base at Lyon-Bron in early March 1940.

1 There was still no official name for the group of pilots.

2 Signal from Gen. Zając to Col. Pawlikowski, the DIAP Commandant, cc. to *Col* Hug, the French Commander of the DIAP.

The list of Kępiński's squadron's flying personnel was as follows:

HQ	1 *Escadrille*	2 *Escadrille*
Commander Maj. Józef Kępiński	Capt. Antoni Wczelik	Capt. Juliusz Frey
Deputy Commander Capt. Piotr Łaguna	Lt Jan Obuchowski	Lt Wacław Wilczewski
	Lt Julian Kowalski	Lt Zdzisław Zadroziński
HQ section	Lt Tadeusz Czerwiński	Lt Robert Janota
Capt. Konrad Sadowski	2nd Lt Bronisław Skibiński	2nd Lt Czesław Główczyński
2nd Lt Stanisław Wielgus	2nd Lt Witold Łanowski	2nd Lt Marian Szalewicz
LAC Eugeniusz Hofmann	2nd Lt Marian Łukaszewicz	2nd Lt Jerzy Czerniak
2nd Lt obs. Kazimierz Bernas	2nd Lt Eugeniusz Fiedorczuk	2nd Lt Leon Jaugsch
2nd Lt obs. Antoni Ignaszak	2nd Lt Aleksy Żukowski	2nd Lt Bolesław Gładych
2nd Lt obs. Jan Siwiec	2nd Lt Jerzy Godlewski	2nd Lt Stanisław Czarnecki
LAC Andrzej Kwiecień	2nd Lt Bronisław Kłosin	2nd Lt Tadeusz Bagrowski
	Cad. Off. Mieczysław Rzemyk	Cad. Off. Mieczysław Leśniewski
	Cad. Off. Bogusław Gęca	Cad. Off. Edward Jaworski
	Cad. Off. Roman Łobarzewski	Cad. Off. Antoni Widawski
	Cad. Off. Tadeusz Pytlak	Cad. Off. Stanislaw Blok
	Cad. Off. Antoni Zieliński	Cad. Off. Aleksander Wlazło
	Cad. Off. Zbigniew Wojda	Cad. Off. Eugeniusz Kropiwnicki
	Cpl Antoni Siudak	Cad. Off. Bronisław Mach
	Cpl Lucjan Szempliński	Cpl Edward Paterek
	Cpl Marian Wędzik	Cpl Jan Palak
	LAC Mieczysław Parafiński	LAC Jerzy Zieliński
	LAC Piotr Zaniewski	LAC Ernest Watolski
	LAC Bolesław Turzański	LAC Edward Uchto
	LAC Józef Derma	LAC Andrzej Niewiara

At the same time, there was a change of concept as to the organisational status of the newly formed squadron. The establishment of the unit was determined at the time, as consistent with the organisation of a Type I single-seat fighter squadron: T.E.G. No. 41 – Fasc. IV. There was a small modification compared to the establishment of a typical French unit of the type: an increased number of officer pilots and a reduced number of NCOs. This was due to the excess of trained officers at DIAP Lyon.

In addition, it was decided to allocate French liaison staff to the establishment number of Polish personnel (an air or ground crew officer, an interpreter officer, an interpreter NCO, a supplies NCO, a clerk private to work in the squadron administration).

The official name of the unit appeared for the first time on that occasion. Gen. Picard wrote: "This squadron will have no. 1/145 and will be detached from the Base (DIAP) at Lyon (Battalion de l'Air No. 145)".

Thus, on 6 April, a new name of the Polish III Fighter Squadron was introduced. It should be noted that the number of the squadron used Arabic numerals from the very beginning, rather than Roman-Arabic as was usual in the French Air Force.

Many authors who write about GC 1/145 stubbornly repeat this obvious error, even forming their own theories for this. This is unnecessary because the official document leaves no doubt.

The squadron was to be formed at the Lyon-Bron base. Each *escadrille* was allocated appropriate means of transport (a liaison car, four 2.5-tonne lorries, an armament trailer, an

[42]: Aircraft of French units at the Lyon-Bron airfield on 27 March 1940. Morane Saulnier MS.406 code no. 7 of the Fighter Training Squadron is in the foreground. (MLP coll.)

42

43

[43]: Morane Saulnier MS.406 c/n 907 (L-936), with code no. 5 applied on a red disc on the fin. The photo was taken after the Germans captured the Lyon-Bron airfield. German soldiers can be seen near the aeroplane. (B. Belcarz coll.)

air heater trailer, a standard trailer, a motorcycle, a bicycle). All the equipment was to be gathered at the base, and the unit was set to achieve combat capability on 5 May 1940. The air crew of the new unit was to be formed primarily from volunteers from the group of Maj. Kępiński, and then from pilots who had already undergone training on the MS 406 at Lyon. Initially, it was the MS 406 that was considered as the equipment of the newly formed unit. This is also evidenced by the fact that the technical staff was picked according to their training on this aircraft type.

Once formed, the *escadrilles* were going to be attached to French units for operational training, just the way it had earlier been with the pilots of the 'Montpellier Escadrille'. Upon their return from the training, the squadron would be formally established by connecting with the engineering and administrative staff at the disposal of the French HQ at Lyon-Bron. A preliminary report on the unit readiness was scheduled for 30 April, and the final report on the preparedness for combat capability was to be presented on 10 May 1940.

On 2 May 1940 the full name of the GC 1/145 was created as "Groupe de chasse Polonais de Varsovie No. 1/145".

As early as in April, there were further rumours about the squadron. It was speculated that the unit would be sent as part of the expeditionary corps to Norway, but the idea was eventually never realised. The German attack on France, which took place on 10 May 1940, resulted in many changes at Lyon. It disturbed the forming of the unit.

The Lyon airfield was attacked by German bombers, which led to the move of the unit to St Symphorien d'Ozon (Lyon-Mions).

Selecting the type of aircraft for the Polish unit was an important issue. In fact, the GC 1/145 still did not have its eventual aeroplanes (the Bloch MB.152 was the first choice), awaiting their allocation. By the 12 May 1940 decision of the French Aviation Ministry, the squadron pilots were to train temporarily on the CR.714 with the temporary task of defending Lyon air space. Only MS.406 aircraft from the DIAP Lyon were fit for this purpose. The Caudrons used at the base were not armed. The deployment to Mions was really a transition to war footing. The pilots were organised as patrols to scramble in emergency.

Around 15 May there were rumours about a change of plans of the French HQ. The GC 1/145, which had not yet reached combat capability, was to be disbanded, and the personnel split into individual *escadrilles* and posted as reinforcements to French units. However, bitter opposition of the Polish side and the support of *Cne* Pierre Rougevin Baville (the French commander of the DIAP Fighter Training Flight) led to the abandonment of this idea. It was decided that the pilots of the DIAP Training Flight would remain at the Mions airfield, while the GC 1/145 would be deployed to the front line.

The move of the to Villacoublay

The decision to move the squadron from Lyon to Villacoublay was made on 17 May 1940. The whole unit was split into three parties. Accordingly, Col Hug, the French commander of the DIAP, appointed a group of sixteen pilots, four of whom were to leave in the first four CR.714s expected from Guyancourt, while the other twelve would depart by air or by road to collect the aeroplanes. This group consisted of the following pilots led by Capt. Antoni Wczelik: Lt Jan Obuchowski, Lt Julian Kowalski, Lt Tadeusz Czerwiński, 2nd Lt Bronisław Skibiński, 2nd Lt Witold Łanowski, 2nd Lt Marian Łukaszewicz, 2nd Lt Aleksy Żukowski, 2nd Lt Eugeniusz Fiedorczuk, 2nd Lt Jerzy Godlewski, Cpl Antoni Siudak, Cpl Marian Wędzik, Cpl Lucjan Szempliński, Cpl Antoni Markiewicz, LAC Mieczysław Parafiński, LAC Piotr Zaniewski.[1]

However, Cpl Antoni Siudak was sent to hospital for treatment and did not return to the unit. Cpl Marian Wędzik was also posted away from the GC 1/145. Eventually Lt Jan Obuchowski, 2nd Lt Marian Łukaszewicz, Cpl Antoni Markiewicz and LAC Mieczysław Parafiński from the group left by train.[2]

Capt. Antoni Wczelik, Lt Tadeusz Czerwiński and Cpl Piotr Zaniewski ferried the following Caudrons, which had reached Mions on 17 May for the GC 1/145: c/n 8540 (I-198), c/n 8544 (I-202) and c/n 8576 (I-234). These three CR.714s were ferried by air on 18 May 1940 (departing at 12.00). The fourth CR.714, c/n 8583 (I-241), reached Villacoublay from Lyon on 21 May 1940. It is highly probable that this machine was a replacement for CR.714 c/n 8581 (I-239) damaged on 17 May 1940[3], ferried by air to Mions by Cpl Marian Wędzik.

The largest group of 162 people (including two Frenchmen) departed by train at 23.30 on 18 May. Capt. Józef Grzebalski commanded the rail party in five railway cars. Maj. Józef Kępiński, the GC 1/145 Commander, also travelled with this party.

The road party, consisting of 48 officers and men (including two Frenchmen), departed the next day at 4.00, under the command of Capt. Adam Jaworski.

1 PI&SM, LOT IV 2/2C1

2 In the group of Capt. Józef Grzebalski.

3 CR.714 c/n 8581 (I-239) was forced to land near Villars-les-Dombes, 25 km north-east of Lyon. The accident was described earlier, with the CR.714 incidents at DIAP, becuse the accident records were prepared at DIAP Lyon-Bron. The aeroplane was salvaged to the base at Bron on 18 May, at the time when three CR.714s departed to Villacoublay, so it was logical that the accident documentation was made at DIAP rather than the GC 1/145, because the aeroplane was never officially taken on charge by the latter unit. C/n 8581 (I-239) was never made airworthy again and it eventually fell into German hands when they captured Lyon.

[44]: GC 1/145 pilots somewhere in France. Standing, left to right: 2nd Lt Bolesław Gładych, 2nd Lt Leon Jaugsch, 2nd Lt Marian Łukaszewicz. Seated, left to right: 2nd Lt Jerzy Czerniak, Lt Zdzisław Zadroziński, Lt Tadeusz Czerwiński, Capt. Juliusz Frey, 2nd Lt Bronisław Skibiński, 2nd Lt Aleksy Żukowski. (B. Belcarz coll.)

Villacoublay

The rail party reached Villacoublay on 19 May 1940, joined there the next day by the road party. The first daily orders of the unit were issued on 20 May, defining administrative and logistics activities for the next day.

Upon arrival, the GC 1/145 was included in the Groupement de Chasse No. 23 with the task of protecting Villacoublay airfield and the southern sector of Paris. The commencement of service was possible only after aircraft were received. In administrative terms, the GC 1/145 reported to Compagnie de l'Air 46/104 under *Lt. de réserve* Gillod. The unit, stationed at Bièvres, also serviced the GC I/4.[4]

Deliveries of aircraft started already on 21 May 1940, when sixteen new Caudrons were received from the factory, increasing the unit's inventory to twenty aircraft. Two more Caudrons were delivered to the squadron on 22 May, and these were assigned to the unit commander Maj. Józef Kępiński and his deputy Capt. Piotr Łaguna.

4 *Lt Col* Salesse (ed.): *L'aviation polonaise en France 1939-40*, p. 121

Aircraft deliveries for the GC 1/145 at the Villacoublay airfield (20/05–2/06/1940):

Date	Military serial no.	Under-wing no. (*Matricule Militaire*)	Construction no.	Allocation	Notes
18/05/1940	8	I-198	8540	2 *Esc.*	DIAP
18/05/1940	12	I-202	8544	2 *Esc.*	DIAP
18/05/1940	44	I-234	8576	2 *Esc.*	DIAP, 27/05/1940 damaged during landing at Villacoublay
21/05/1940	51	I-241	8583	2 *Esc.*	DIAP
21/05/1940	40	I-230	8572	1 *Esc.*	25/05/1940 collision CR.714 c/n 8580
21/05/1940	46	I-236	8578	1 *Esc.*	
21/05/1940	43	I-233	8575	1 *Esc.*	
21/05/1940	50	I-240	8582	1 *Esc.*	
21/05/1940	36	I-226	8568	1 *Esc.*	
21/05/1940	45	I-235	8577	1 *Esc.*	
21/05/1940	48	I-238	8580	1 *Esc.*	25/05/1940 collision CR.714 c/n 8572
21/05/1940	34	I-224	8566	1 *Esc.*	
21/05/1940	11	I-201	8543	2 *Esc.*	
21/05/1940	32	I-222	8564	2 *Esc.*	
21/05/1940	31	I-221	8563	2 *Esc.*	24/05/1940 collision MS. 230 c/n 574
21/05/1940	19	I-209	8551	2 *Esc.*	
21/05/1940	39	I-229	8571	2 *Esc.*	
21/05/1940	24	I-214	8556	2 *Esc.*	
21/05/1940	23	I-213	8555	2 *Esc.*	
22/05/1940	33	I-223	8565	HQ section	Kępiński
22/05/1940	22	I-212	8554	HQ section	Łaguna
26/05/1940	10	I-200	8542	2 *Esc.*	
26/05/1940	52	I-242	8584	2 *Esc.*	
26/05/1940	30	I-220	8562	2 *Esc.*	
28/05/1940	1	I-191	8533	1 *Esc.*	
28/05/1940	56	I-246	8588	1 *Esc.*	
28/05/1940	17	I-207	8549	1 *Esc.*	
28/05/1940	18	I-208	8550	1 *Esc.*	
28/05/1940	47	I-237	8579	1 *Esc.*	
28/05/1940	20	I-210	8552	2 *Esc.*	
29/05/1940	41	I-231	8573	1 *Esc.*	
29/05/1940	[illegible]	I-22[illegible]	[illegible]	2 *Esc.*	
30/05/1940	37	I-227	8569	1 *Esc.*	
30/05/1940	54	I-244	8586	2 *Esc.*	
30/05/1940	53	I-243	8585	2 *Esc.*	
30/05/1940	38	I-228	8570	2 *Esc.*	
2/06/1940	55	I-245	8587	2 *Esc.*	Wreck at Villacoublay. Godlewski
8/06/1940	57	I-247	8589		de Marmier

[45]: The fuselage of CR.714 c/n 8576 (I-234) less the engine section, with the removed wing placed alongside. On 27 May 1940, this aeroplane was damaged by 2nd Lt Fiedorczuk, who forgot to lower the undercarriage when coming in to land. (T. Rajkowski coll.)

The first days were quite calm, apart from the incidents that involved the loss of the newly-obtained aircraft. Caudron-Renault CR.714 c/n 8563 (I-221) was lost already three days after it was taken on charge by the unit. The incident occurred on 24 May 1940 at Villacoublay. Morane Saulnier MS.230 c/n 574, taxiing to take off for a training flight, hit the fuselage of the parked CR.714 c/n 8563.

Thus, the first aeroplane was struck off charge of the GC 1/145. The unfortunate series continued. Another incident occurred the next day, this time with the participation of two CR.714s from the GC 1/145. 2nd Lt Fiedorczuk landed at Villacoublay about 20.30, returning from a patrol in CR.714 c/n 8580 (I-238). During taxiing, he turned to avoid collision with a Curtis H 75 and collided with CR.714 c/n 8572 (I-230, serial no. 40). The propeller and the front part of the fuselage of Fiedorczuk's aeroplane were damaged, while c/n 8572 was damaged at the central section of the fuselage near the cockpit. The pilot was uninjured. The accident was caused by limited visibility during taxiing.

Polish national markings and code numbers appeared on the new aeroplanes at Villacoublay.

2nd Lt Eugeniusz Fiedorczuk damaged CR.714 c/n 8576 (I-234) on 27 May 1940 morning. When coming in to land, he forgot to lower the undercarriage. The pilot escaped without serious injury. It must be admitted that Fiedorczuk was exceptionally unfortunate with the CR.714. This was already at least the third machine of the type that he damaged.

The stay at Villacoublay was a period of hard work. The subsequent CR.714s taken on charge required a lot of work. Information about the difficulties in obtaining spare parts, a lack of tools and a limited involvement of factory specialists appears in many accounts.

Col. Stefan Pawlikowski, who had meanwhile ceased to be the commander of the DIAP Lyon, joined the GC 1/145 at Villacoublay on 23 May. Apart from him, French officers joined the unit: *Cne* Maurice Bessault (on 24 May from the base at Rennes) and Cdt Alexandre Lionel de Marmier (on 27 May from the DIAP Lyon).

On 24 May, at the request of the Aviation Minister, Maj. Kępiński met Col Domino, the administrative commander of the *Secteur de l'Air* no. 51 to determine the details of the squadron inspection.

The same day, the GC 1/145 was visited at Villacoublay by Gen. Józef Zając, the Polish Air Force Commander. He recalled it as follows in his memoirs: "I have inspected the 145 Fighter Squadron moved from Lyon to the Villacoublay airfield near Paris. Maj. Kępiński is the Commander, Capt. Łaguna his deputy. An air raid alert occurs during the inspection. The sqn does not have the full number of 'Caudron 714' aircraft yet. I found Villacoublay air defence completely unprepared. I have influenced the French commander of the airfield towards organising such defence and participation of our fighter squadron in this defence".[5] The next day, Gen. Zając informed Gen. Władysław Sikorski, the Polish Commander-in-Chief, about the situation of the Polish Air Force, including the deployment of the GC 1/145.

The meeting with Col Domino on 24 May resulted in an inspection on 29 May 1940. A report was prepared at the time,

5 Józef Zając, *Dwie wojny*, London 1964 p. 367

[16]: Damaged Caudron CR.714 c/n 8587 (I-245) in the SNCAN hangar at Villacoublay. According to GC 1/145 documents it had been delivered to the unit on 2 June 1940 and allocated to the 2 Esc. It was probably this aeroplane that was damaged on 10 June during attempted take-off from Villacoublay with 2nd Lt Godlewski at the controls. Note the absence of code number and cut-outs in the covering on the wing, where the small roundel had been, and on the fuselage (where the Polish marking may have been). (B. Belcarz coll.)

which has listed a number of problems related mainly to the Caudron-Renault CR.714s. The most common complaints against the GC 1/145 aeroplanes included problems with the undercarriage mechanism, the starters, the adjustable propeller pitch mechanism and the engine overheating. The report concluded that the pilots expected deliveries of a better type of fighter, capable of fighting.[6]

6 Some accounts claim that the Aviation Minister performed it himself and that the Polish pilots decided to continue flying the Caudrons at their own risk after flights on the type were suspended, allegedly. In fact the visit was made by a representative of the minister, *Col* Domino, and the Poles, despite real reluctance of many pilots towards the Caudron, had no real prospect of receiving a new fighter type. On 5 June, Gen. Zając, when analysing the equipment used by the Poles, said: "the

Delivery date	*1 Escadrille*	*2 Escadrille*	HQ
18/05/1940 from Villacoublay via Lyon-Bron	8576 (44) I-234	8540 (8) I-198 8544 (12) I-202	
21/05/1940 from DIAP		8583 (51) I-241	
21/05/1940 from Villacoublay	8566 (34) I-224 8568 (36) I-226 8572 (40) I-230 8575 (43) I-233 8577 (45) I-235 8578 (46) I-236 8580 (48) I-238 8582 (50) I-240	8543 (11) I-201 8551 (19) I-209 8555 (23) I-213 8556 (24) I-214 8564 (32) I-222 8571 (39) I-229	8563 (31) I-221[1]
22/05/1940 from Villacoublay			8565 (33) I-223 commander 8554 (22) I-212 deputy commander
26/05/1940 from Villacoublay		8542 (10) I-200 8562 (30) I-220 8584 (52) I-242	
28/05/1940 from Villacoublay	8533 (1) I 191 8549 (17) I-207 8550 (18) I-208 8579 (47) I-237 8588 (56) I-246	8552 (20) I-210	
29/05/1940 from Villacoublay	8573 (41) I-231	8567 (35) I-225	
30/05/1940 from Villacoublay	8569 (37) I-227	8570 (38) I-228 8585 (53) I-243 8586 (54) I-244	
2/06/1940 from Villacoublay		8587 (25) I-245	
8/06/1940			8589 (57) I-247 de Marmier
Total	16	18	4

1 Machine not allocated officially to any of the *Escadrilles*, damaged 24 May 1940.

Formally[7] the GC 1/145 has commenced operational activity on 28 May 1940 at 12.00. The following day, Gen. Pinsard, commanding the Groupement de Chasse No. 21, received orders[8] from Gen. d'Astier, commanding the Zone d'Operations Aériennes Nord, that notified him about subordinating the GC 1/145 to the Groupement de Chasse No. 21 and ordering evacuation of the unit from the overcrowded base at Villacoublay as soon as possible.

Guyancourt, where the Caudron assembly plant was located, was to be the new location of the unit. However, due to absence of any logistics facilities to allow effective operational activity, Gen. Pinsard replaced Guyancourt with Dreux on 30 May, setting the new date of the unit's move at 31 May 1940. For technical reasons, the date of the move was then postponed again, to 2 June 1940.

At the same time the GC 1/145 saw some personnel changes. Cpl Antoni Siudak and Cpl Marian Wędzik left it, as described earlier. 2nd Lt Witold Łanowski was the last pilot to leave it, when he was sentenced to a disciplinary penalty of 21 days of strict detention for disseminating unfounded accusations against his superior officer.

On 2 June 1940, the squadron moved westward from Villacoublay, to Dreux. The next day, Villacoublay airfield was bombed. The squadron left the base near Paris with 34 aircraft on charge (31 CR.714s flew to Dreux that day). However, lack of proper technical facilities hampered the maintenance. In order to improve the operations of GC 1/145, two officers were sent to the unit: Col. Stefan Pawlikowski (temporarily at the disposal of the Groupement de Chasse No. 21 that was part of the Zone d'Operations Aériennes Nord) and Cdt Alexandre Lionel de Marmier (from DIAP Lyon-Bron). Pawlikowski was going to be an advisor, while de Marmier was a technical advisor who also acted as Kępiński's deputy[9].

Following the departure of four pilots, the incomplete GC 1/145 flying personnel required reinforcement. According to a letter from the French Aviation Ministry of 29 May 1940[10] Col Hug issued orders no. 5349/S/D.I. the following day, which listed those who were going to join the squadron: three pilots and two interpreters. 2nd Lt Zbigniew Wróblewski, Cpl Ladislav Uher (Czech) and LAC Antoni Joda were the pilots while 2nd Lt Ludwik Dziadosz and 2nd Lt Stefan Stenocki, the interpreters[11]. They left Lyon on 30 May evening and reached Villacoublay the next day. Wróblewski was posted to the 2 Esc., while Joda and Uher to the 1 Esc. of the GC 1/145.

'Caudrons' and 'Moranes' are to be rejected. If we cannot get the 'Curtisses', then 'Bloch 152s' and maybe 'Koolhovens', that our pilots praise, are better than those".

7 Machine not allocated officially to any of the *Escadrilles*, damaged 24 May 1940.

8 Telephone-gram no. 884-3/OS/EMG of 27 May 1940.

9 Orders no. 1839-S/3-0

10 Orders no. 1957 1/1S of 28 May 1940 named 2 June 1940 as the day of de Marmier's posting.

11 No. 1978 E.M.A.A. 1/1.

Dreux

2 June

In the morning the squadron was still at Villacoublay. Orders from the HQ of the Groupement de Chasse No. 21 reached the unit there about 13.20:

1) If there are attacks on the Paris region, one of the *escadrilles* will scramble to protect the Villacoublay area. The duty should be carried out for about 30 minutes.
2) After the duty is carried out, the *escadrille*'s aircraft will land at the new airfield (Dreux).
3) During the operation, the other *escadrille* will be in a state of combat readiness.
4) If the second *escadrille* enters action then, following completion of its duty, it will perform the same cross country flight as the first *escadrille*.
5) If no defensive action is performed, the move will take place at 16.00.[12]

The move to Dreux took place on the afternoon of 2 June 1940. The aeroplanes were ready for the flight from 3.45 a.m. The air party had no problem with the move, because the distance between Villacoublay and Dreux was about 65 km. However, covering this distance proved a big problem for the road party of the squadron, which has only arrived there in the evening of 2 June, going through overcrowded roads. Two RAF squadrons, a Hurricane and a bomber ones, were based at the airfield. The Poles met withdrawing elements of the Air Component of the British Expeditionary Force commanded by A/Cdre John Beresford Cole-Hamilton. For several days the airfield at Dreux has been the place where the RAF tried to reorganise their units that had become separated during the withdrawal.

Upon arrival at Dreux the GC 1/145 was organisationally linked with the French GC II/1 squadron, based since 2 June at Brétigny airfield (commanded by Cdt Robillon).

One Caudron was lost during the move, which may have resulted from a pilot error when landing or from the condition of the airfield surface. The conditions that the Poles found at Dreux were difficult, the NCOs and men were billeted in the buildings of the surrounding farms, while the officers resided

12 Stenocki was also a cipher clerk.

in a hotel at Dreux. Catering left much to be desired (a French field kitchen), while the sanitary conditions for the NCOs and men were appalling by any standards. A part of maintenance workshops for the aeroplanes were hidden in a wood near the airfield. After a few hours at Dreux, the Poles were offered assistance by the British.

3 June

From the early morning work continued at the airfield to adapt it to the needs of the unit and to prepare aircraft for possible action. About 9.00 a.m., information was received at the airfield from the Groupement de Chasse No. 21 that ordered combat readiness for 'a double patrol' (two sections, i.e. six aircraft, one section from each *escadrille*) for air protection of the area around the airfield. From 13.00 two sections from the 1 Esc. were on alert, while the entire 2 Esc. was supposed to be 'waiting' ('attendre').

The absence of a squadron radio was a major obstacle, necessitating ancient methods of communication. Pilots patrolling the vicinity of the airfield were to receive information about the direction of German aeroplanes by means of sheets laid out on the ground.

About a quarter past 13.00, the squadron received conflicting orders sent by the Groupements de Chasse No. 21 and 23. As a result, a section from the 1 Esc.[13] was scrambled and patrolled the Dreux area for about 50 minutes at an altitude of 5,000 m. The second scramble that day took place later in the afternoon. The Chartres area was patrolled. On 3 June evening the GC 1/145 had 27 serviceable aeroplanes.

Throughout the day Cdt de Marmier tried to improve the functioning of the squadron by complementing its technical means. In a report he made a few days later, he clearly indicated that throughout the time the GC 1/145 was left without any coherent instructions that would allow it to operate autonomously. The 3 June 1940 report of the Groupement de Chasse No. 21 recorded no combats fought by GC 1/145 pilots.[14]

4 June

On the night of 3 June the unit received telephone information from the Groupement de Chasse No. 21 that due to an expected German attack, the squadron should maintain one *escadrille* at combat readiness from 4.15 a.m. for air defence of own territory, while the other would be prepared to provide support for stronger defence.

That day, a radio station reached Dreux, thanks to which it was possible to abandon the ancient methods of communication (signs laid out on the ground) and organise radio communication. However, the time of transferring information from the warning network (from the Eiffel tower) was usually delayed by 6 to 10 minutes.[15] One patrol by six aircraft was flown above the airfield that day. No enemy aeroplanes were encountered.

Maj. Kępiński has used a period of relative calm to inspect the airfield area. This resulted in issuing guidelines on how to camouflage aircraft and equipment. The directive also discussed the camouflaging of airfield defence anti-aircraft artillery positions.

On 4 June evening the GC 1/145 had 24 serviceable aeroplanes.

5 June

The Germans broke the French defence line. The assault was accompanied by intensified air operations, both in the front line area and further inland. That day at 5.25 the GC 1/145 was ordered to send one *escadrille* to Rouen. There is no information available to confirm that these orders have been carried out.[16]

However, new orders were received at 6.30, this time to move one *escadrille* to the Bretigny-sur-Orge airfield, for air defence of Paris. The GC 1/145 was to support the GC II/1 that was based at that airfield. The 1 Esc. flew to Bretigny. After refuelling, the *escadrille* flew a 45 minute patrol over Paris (at an altitude of 6,000 m) and landed again at Bretigny. All aeroplanes then returned to Dreux. The GC 1/145 flew no more sorties that day. In the evening, 21 aeroplanes and 33 pilots were available for the next day.

6 June

The situation at the front line became bad for the French. The Germans broke through their lines in many places and, as a result, the main task for the French fighter force on 6 June 1940 was to defend their own troops and escort bombers to attack the enemy. The GC 1/145 displayed relatively little activity that day. Aircraft of the unit flew six combat sorties. The CR.714s of the Polish unit were to defend the area of Berney. Communications improved on 6 June. 1,300 m of telephone cable was received from the base at Chartres, which made it possible to connect the airfield at Dreux with the warning network station. In addition, the Compagnie de l'Air 46/104 arrived at the airfield with an anti-aircraft section which had a battery of three 25 mm cannon and four batteries of twinned M.A.C. machine guns. The HQ of Compagnie de l'Air 46/104 was located at Vernouillet. It controlled elements of the

13 *Lt Col* Salesse (ed.): *L'aviation polonaise en France 1939-40*, p. 234

14 Including the section no. 4 of .Lt J. Kowalski.

15 It is difficult to find corroboration for de Marmier's victories (1 confirmed + 1 probable credited by the French). There are two reasons for that: 1) no corroboration for de Marmier flying that day, 2) his efforts to cure the numerous administrative problems encountered in the functioning of the squadron at the new location, which required his presence at the airfield.

16 An aircraft flying over Paris could get to Dreux area during such time period.

Détachement de transmissions 23/705 and the Compagnie de Combustibles Liquides 32/125.[17]

At 11.30 p.m., Maj. Kępiński was informed by phone that from the following day the squadron would be transferred organisationally from Groupement de Chasse No. 21 to report to the Sous-Groupement No. 42[18] based at Mantes, commanded by Lt Col Augier de Moussac. The Sous-Groupement had already included the GC I/4 (Evreux) and GC III/3 (Illiers – L'Evêque), and now, in addition to the GC 1/145, it was also joined by the GC II/10 (Berney) and GC III/10 (Deauville). Sous-Groupement de Chasse No. 42 transferred to report to Groupement de Chasse No. 23, commanded by Gen. Romatet.

7 June

There is no full documentation of GC 1/145 combat activity in the morning hours that day. The report prepared by the GC 1/145 commander includes sorties flown in the afternoon. That day, the GC 1/145 began patrolling the Seine at the sector of the Xe Armée Terrestre. Without knowing the activity of the squadron in the morning, it can be stated that its CR.714s flew at least two patrols this day.

Between 15.40 and 16.30, two sections of three aeroplanes each patrolled the area of Houdan–Meulan–Magny–Flevry–Vernon at 6,500 m. The operation was uneventful. The next operation was flown in the evening, between 19.00 and 21.15. This time two three-aeroplane sections patrolled the area of Dreux–Mantes–Seine–Vernon–Dreux at 6,500–7,000 m. This flight was also uneventful. Forest fires were seen about 30 km north of the patrolled area.

17 Report of 5 June indicates that the GC 1/145 has flown 13 sorties that day, which suggests only one *Escadrille* was active.

18 *Lt Col* Salesse (ed.): *L'aviation polonaise en France 1939-40*, p. 231

8 June

That day, German troops made a breach between the X and VII Armies south of Poix, advancing towards Rouen. The role of the French Air Force was to slow down the enemy attack. Fighter units, including the GC 1/145, were to provide air cover. At about 10.00, four sections flew to the Berney airfield, becoming subordinated to the commander of the GC II/10. Between 11.28 and 12.30 the Caudrons performed a patrol at an altitude of 5,000-6,000 m without contact with the enemy. Also the next mission (scramble) flown by five aircraft (between 13.30 and 14.30) was uneventful. The operation was similar to that in the morning: a patrol at 5,500-6,000 m.

The baptism of fire took place in the afternoon. Five aircraft from the 1 Esc. were scrambled at 15.54. The mission was flown by the following pilots: Capt. Wczelik (code no. 3), Lt Czerwiński (7), 2nd Lt Godlewski (2), 2nd Lt Żukowski (13), Cpl Zaniewski (15). The aeroplanes headed towards the Seine and then flew towards Rouen, over which explosions of shells

[47]: The aeroplanes withdrawn from service with the GC 1/145 for technical reasons were very carefully camouflaged at the edge of the Dreux copse. The photo shows an unidentified Caudron, with c/n 8578 (I-236) and probably c/n 8569 (I-227) behind it. The photo was taken about 15 June 1940, after the Germans had captured the airfield but before they began repositioning the aeroplanes there. (B. Belcarz coll.)

[48]: Reconstruction of the Dreux airfield location. The enlarged section shows the positions of aeroplanes in the so-called 'Caudron Avenue', after the Germans captured the airfield. (Reconstruction by Thierry Vallet according to the author's guidelines.)

were observed. About an hour into the flight, at an altitude of about 4,000 m, a group of Messerschmitt Bf 110s was encountered and engaged. The combat took place south-west of Rouen about 16.50. According to the squadron report, a group of about twenty Messerschmitt Bf 110s were encountered in the air. The same document credits a Bf 110 probably shot down to Capt. Wczelik and Lt Czerwiński.[19] The Polish section was vastly outnumbered by the Germans, which put the Poles in a difficult position. However, the Germans did not engage and broke away from the attacking Caudrons.[20] In result of the combat, at least three aeroplanes landed at the Evreux airfield. The 9 June 1940 report that discussed the activities of the previous day included the information that "one of our aeroplanes was damaged due to a hole in the engine resulting from the impact of bullets. It got 30 bullets."[21] The damaged aeroplane was CR.714 c/n 8549 (I-207), which remained at the airfield, where it was then captured by the Germans. Relatively many photos of this machine survive, but none show traces of German bullets. There must have been other reasons for leaving it at Evreux.

On 8 June, there was a lot of speculation regarding further independent existence of the GC 1/145. This was thought to originate in the circles of the French Aviation Ministry.[22] Gen. Ujejski reported that day to Gen. Zając that Gen. Pinsard, commanding the fighter force, was dissatisfied with the Polish squadron. The arguments raised by the French focused on the following theses:

1) the aeroplanes used by the GC 1/145 were not suitable for combat use;
2) therefore, the squadron was unable to make its mark among other fighter squadrons;
3) there were difficulties with leading the squadron due to the insufficient command of French by Polish commanders
4) it would be more expedient to split the Polish flying personnel and post them to French Air Force units to fill the vacancies among French personnel.

Gen. Zając told Gen.Ujejski to immediately meet both Gen. Pinsard and Gen. Picard in connection with this information. At the same time, Col. Pawlikowski came to the Polish HQ in Paris and his explanations helped, in part, to learn the

19 *Sous-Groupement de Chasse No. 42* was re-formed from *Groupement de Chasse No. 25*, which took place on 20 May 1940.

20 M. Comas, a French historian, has found information at the Bundesarchiv that confirms the loss of a Messerschmitt Bf 110 of the III./ZG 26 on 8 June 1940 in the Rouen-Boos area. In his opinion this victory can be credited to the GC 1/145.

21 This is a puzzling fact. One may guess that the Germans had another important task and did not want to engage the five CR.714s, or that they had little fuel left for the return to base.

22 *GC 1/145. Compte rendus special du 8 VI – 9 VI au midi.*

sources of this situation. He said that the Commander of the Sous-Groupement de Chasse No. 42 asked for posting of Polish pilots to French units, with support from Gen. d'Astier, commanding the Zone d'Operations Aériennes Nord (the Zone being equivalent to an air army). It should be assumed that the arguments about a lack of success of the Poles were a pretext, as it turned out that Gen. Pinsard had no comments for the actions of the GC 1/145.

Before he visited the HQ, Col. Pawlikowski has acquainted officers of the squadron with the same arguments. In reply to this information the squadron commander, Maj. Kępiński, wrote a letter addressed to Gen. Zając. He described his point of view as follows: "I report, sir, that I am in clear contradiction both to the form and the content of the motives communicated by Col. Pawlikowski. If the raison d'etat and the position of the Polish Air Force requires that, and you find it appropriate to disband the unit, I will surrender to that without reservations. However, I believe that it is wrong for me and all the officers to be involved in discussions on this subject. Personally, I do not think that in this battle the success of the Allies depends on one air unit, or rather on its disbandment. (...) I cannot report to you, sir, that the aircraft we have are at the required level, but one can fight even with these aeroplanes, knowing in advance that although the successes will not be great, the only Polish air unit will be maintained. Many of our pilots are already with French units, and each of them waits for the moment when he will be able to serve in a Polish unit."[23]

The allegations of the French side were a reaction to de Marmier's report rather than a reliable assessment of the situation. Perhaps it was easier for de Marmier to draw conclusions

23 The Aviation Ministry received a report from Cdt de Marmier of 7 June 1940, in which he wrote: "I think it has to be indicated to you, after a few days of mutual work, that the unit, composed of valuable staff, will not be able, under these conditions, to be as effective as we have the right to expect... We ascertain that the effectiveness of a pilot will be about 70% less than that of his colleagues placed in French escadrilles... These men, with a Slavonic nature, are unable to understand the important role that is given to them, they see the war from the viewpoint of their private war. Example: unable to follow the schedule of activities, we should expect various delays, from 30–40 minutes in patrol scramble." Report of Cdt de Marmier for the Aviation Minister (HQ of the *Armée de l'Air 1ᵉ Bureau*). SHAA Archives Paris. The report was then forwarded (letter no. 2865-I/1-C/E.M.A.A. of 8 June 1940) by the Aviation Minister to the Supreme Commander of the Air Force with the following comments: "I have the honour to send you in attachment a copy of the report of Commandant de Marmier, a French officer attached to the Polish I/145 unit. The report includes an assessment of the dangers to which we are exposed, if we start too quickly and without preparation of the Polish HQ to realise the requests of Gen. Zając regarding the forming of Polish units... The requests have been forwarded to me and repeated with pressure, but current conditions make them inappropriate... If you receive other reports (similar to the report of *Cdt* de Marmier) from commanders who have Polish units under their command, these should be kept, which can be useful to present them to Gen. Zając."

[49]: CR.714 fighters from the 2 Escadrille *of the GC 1/145 after the Germans entered the Dreux airfield: c/n 8543, code no. 10 (I-201) of LAC Niewiara, c/n 8544, code no. 13 (I-202) of 2nd Lt Gładych and c/n 8555, code no. 7 (I-213) of Lt Zadroziński. (P. Tuliński coll.)*

49

[50]: The same group of aircraft photographed by the Germans just after they entered Dreux: code nos. 13 of Gładych, 7 of Zadroziński, and 10 of Niewiara. (B. Belcarz coll.)

that emphasized the Poles' lack of preparedness for combat than to admit that organisation was failing, the latter putting the blame on the French side.[24]

As a result of the conference held by Gen. Zając with Col. Pawlikowski, the Polish Air Force Commander decided to meet Gen. d'Astier to demand that: "…he assigns one *escadrille* to a French squadron while the other remains, and the squadron, following the battle that awaits it, will be reunited into one whole."[25] According to Gen. Zając, this was the only way out to enable the unit to remain independent. The meeting with Gen. d'Astier took place on 9 June at Nogent sur Seine. After discussions with Gen. d'Arcourt, the Fighter Force Inspector, Gen. d'Astier agreed with the proposal of the Polish side, which in fact followed the French demands.[26] It can be called a "Solomon judgment" because the postulates of both parties have been partially implemented.

9 June

That morning about 5.00, three light sections (nine Caudrons) moved to the Berney airfield.[27] They flew a one-hour patrol (6.30–7.30) at an altitude of 4,500 m without seeing the enemy. At about the same time (6.40–7.45), a section of the aeroplanes that had remained at Dreux[28] were scrambled to defend the airfield area. This operation, flown at 5,500 m, also ended without contact with the enemy.

That day, the Germans focused on crossing the Seine in its lower section. The oil refineries at Le Havre and Port Jérôme had been on fire since the morning, and the dark smoke significantly limited visibility in the air throughout the region. Eventually, the German plans were successful and on 9/10 June they captured the crossings on the Seine at Rouen and Pont de l'Arche. The development of the situation at this section of the front line resulted in an increased activity of the Allies. The GC 1/145, similar to French squadrons, received subse-

24 The letter was written by Maj. Kępiński on 8 June 1940, the day before the combat when he was seriously wounded. It was, therefore, probably never sent. It expresses, perhaps in a slightly emotional way, but certainly sincerely, his mood when he wrote it. Kępiński had some complexes that resulted from his poor command of the French language. Besides, the fact that Col. Pawlikowski presented the French point of view to squadron pilots was, in a way, questioning Kępiński's position as the commander. Even more so as, being junior in rank to Pawlikowski, he was not in fact able to present directly his opinion on the matter.

25 This part of the story is best concluded with the excellent results soon achieved by Polish fighter pilots in the Battle of Britain.

26 ibid.

27 There actions resulted in the French decision of 12 June 1940 (letter from Gen. d'Astier no. 2144 – S/3-0) to detach two groups of eight people each from the GC 1/145, to be trained on Bloch 152s in two French units: the GC I/1 and GC I/8.

28 *La patrouille legère* (three aircraft), as opposed to *La patrouille lourde* (five aircraft).

51

[51]: The GC 1/145 aeroplanes left by Poles at the Dreux airfield. Morane Saulnier MS.406 c/n 1013 is second left. The picture was taken from the bushes towards the local road to Dreux. (B. Belcarz coll.)

At midday on 9 June[1], the engineering services prepared a report that listed the squadron aircraft:

No.	Allocation	Aircraft serial no.	Engine no.	C/n	troubles/notes
1	HQ	33	35	8565	ready/Kępiński
2	HQ	22	27	8554	ready/Łaguna
3	HQ	57	83	8589	ready/de Marmier
4	1 Esc	46	63	8578	engine supercharger damaged
5	1 Esc	37	69	8569	engine seized
6	1 Esc	45	64	8577	ready
7	1 Esc	43	38	8575	ready
8	1 Esc	36	51	8568	ready
9	1 Esc	34	41	8566	ready
10	1 Esc	50	74	8582	tailplane and elevator replacement
11	1 Esc	12	7	8544	overhaul following a forced landing
12	1 Esc	8	81	8540	ready
13	1 Esc	41	79	8573	ready
14	1 Esc	18	44	8550	forced landed
15	1 Esc	56	73	8588	wheels, tubes, tyres and propeller damaged
16	1 Esc	17	80	8549	forced landed
17	1 Esc	1	66	8533	glazing replacement, damaged wheel
18	1 Esc	47	64	8579	ready
19	2 Esc	35	82	8567	ready
20	2 Esc	52	78	8584	ready
21	2 Esc	20	65	8552	crashed at the front line
22	2 Esc	54	32	8586	ready
23	2 Esc	24	29	8556	engine overhaul (erratic in flight)
24	2 Esc	30	46	8562	ready
25	2 Esc	23	30	8555	ready
26	2 Esc	10	15	8542	ready
27	2 Esc	39	43	8571	ready
28	2 Esc	11	24	8543	ready
29	2 Esc	19	48	8551	repair to the propeller pitch electric system
30	2 Esc	38	39	8570	ready
31	2 Esc	32	52	8564	carburettor replacement
32	2 Esc	51	75	8583	ready
33	2 Esc	53	59	8585	ready
34	2 Esc	25	42	8557	crashed at an airfield

1 The number of aircraft in that sections is not known.

[52]: The 'Caudron Avenue' as seen from the airfield towards the road. Aeroplanes of the 2 Escadrille *are in the foreground (B. Belcarz coll.)*

quent duties over the Seine valley. The Poles were supposed to defend the cities and the sector between Meulan and Rouen.

21 aeroplanes were combat ready. 18 of these were scrambled to patrol the Seine section between Meulan and Rouen. The take-off took place about 14.50. The formation was led by the HQ section (Kępiński, Łaguna, de Marmier).

The complete listing of the formation was as follows:[29]

No.	Pilot/*Escadrille*	C/n	Code no.	Notes
1	Maj. Józef Kępiński	8565	– of the HQ	forced landing at Dreux
2	Capt. Piotr Łaguna	8554	= of the HQ	
3	Cdt. Alexandre L. de Marmier	8589	of the HQ	
4	Capt. Antoni Wczelik		3 of the 1 *Esc.*	
5	Cpl Antoni Markiewicz		1 of the 1 *Esc.*	
6	Lt Julian Kowalski	8573	10 of the 1 *Esc.*	returned to Dreux wounded
7	Lt Jan Obuchowski		4 of the 1 *Esc.*	killed in action
8	2nd Lt Bronisław Skibiński	8566	5 of the 1 *Esc.*	forced landing at Dreux
9	2nd Lt Jerzy Godlewski		? of the 1 *Esc.*	landed at Villacoublay
10	Capt. Juliusz Frey		1 of the 2 *Esc.*	failure, returned to Dreux before the combat
11	2nd Lt Czesław Główczyński	8584	2 of the 2 *Esc.*	
12	2nd Lt Jerzy Czerniak		6 of the 2 *Esc.*	forced landing Dreux?
13	Lt Zdzisław Zadroziński	8555	7 of the 2 *Esc.*	
14	2nd Lt Lech Lachowicki-Czechowicz		14 of the 2 *Esc.*	killed in action
15	Cpl Jan Palak		12 of the 2 *Esc.*	
16	LAC Edward Uchto		8 of the 2 *Esc.*	killed in action
17	LAC Andrzej Niewiara	8543	10 of the 2 *Esc.*	
18	LAC Mieczysław Parafiński		6 of the 1 *Esc.*	

Soon after the take-off, Capt. Frey left the formation, as his Caudron had engine problems. 17 aircraft remained in the formation. Due to technical problems with the radios there was no radio communication between the aeroplanes.[30]

The GC 1/145 reached the designated patrol area in the vicinity of Meulan at an altitude of 6,000 m.

The weather was very good and many *Luftwaffe* aeroplanes operated in the sector. The position for the attack was perfect because the Caudrons were approaching the patrol area out of strong sunlight. The initial phase of the flight is described in the recollections of 2nd Lt Główczyński:

"We flew at about 6,000 m. We crossed the Seine with the sun exactly behind us. I look and I don't believe my eyes: some 2,000 m below us, Messerschmitt 109s in a beautiful formation, just like us. It was an afternoon, the sun that was blazing into our tails was hiding perfectly the stretched arrow of three-aircraft Vics. [...] A dream position to attack, provided to us by a happy coincidence!

"Kępiński, however, flies on as if nothing happened, [...] I approach Kępiński myself. I point down from the cockpit with my hand. He nods, to show that he can see. [...] Then I show to my commander that I am going down at them, and Kępiński, saluting me as a sign of consent, gives his blessing. Godspeed! [...] "I didn't think of anything any more, diving on the Messerschmitts. I didn't even notice that nobody followed me. Even my wingman, Czerniak, only joined me after the Messerschmitt formation split across the sky, saving me. I wasn't hot-headed enough to aim at the German leader. [...] I aimed at a fighter of the starboard section of their entire formation. Those at the front didn't even realise, they were still coming to their senses when their friend was already going down in flames. They split immediately, diving in various direc-

29 The report is incorrectly dated at 8 June 1940. Findings of the author and M. Comas.

30 The listing of aircraft numbers is hypothetic (reconstructed according to the findings of the author and M. Comas).

tions. It was low above the forests around the Seine. I already had one Bf 109; I started chasing another. Then yet another Messerschmitt fired at me, and this one in turn got on my tail. I was hanging on my harness at that moment, chasing the other German, speeding almost vertically to the ground. [...] At that moment, the cockpit kind of got dusty, splinters and pieces of glass flew right under my nose. I got it from the one flying on my tail in the great turmoil. But Czerniak shot him down. The Messerschmitt, however, managed to fire one well-aimed burst. My instruments were damaged, but my colossal war luck smiled at me twice again. First, by sending Czerniak with help and second, by making me getting hit when in that exact position. In the Cyclones we had armoured plates behind us, not too thick, but enough. You had to sit perfectly straight up for them to fulfil their task. Each move to one side brought the pilot out of the protected space. While diving vertically, I was bent forward and perfectly screened along the flight line by this narrow armour plate. I later found out that it was badly damaged by the Messerschmitt's burst."[31]

Due to the attack of Główczyński and Czerniak the III./JG26 formation that escorted the Dornier 17s of the KG2 dispersed. This was used by the remaining GC 1/145 pilots, who attacked the bomber formation. In spite of the attack of Główczyński and Czerniak that dispersed the bomber escort, some of the

31 The problems had existed earlier, but squadron engineering services were unable to cope with these on their own.

9 June 1940, 18.00 hrs

Groupement de Chasse 21
Sous-Groupement de Chasse 42
Groupe de Chasse 1/145

Combat report

Mission:
Destruction of enemy air force with 6 sections over the zone: Vallée de la Seine, from Meulon to Rouen, inclusive.
Performance:
6 sections under the command of *Cdt* Kępiński, spaced from an altitude of 200 m[1] to 5,000 m. Take-off at 14.00. Flying over Meulon, we were fired at by anti-aircraft artillery, similarly at Vernon. Over Vernon there was a combat with about 20 Messerschmitt 109 aircraft that covered bombers (Dornier). Our sections attacked the bombers (Dornier). The combat was prolonged because the radio did not work well and cooperation between the sections became difficult. The combat of a group turned into a combat of sections.
Did not return until 16.30:
S/lieutenant Lachowicki, *Lieutenant* Obuchowski, *Cap-Chef* Uchto.
Pilots who shot down the enemy:
1) *S/lieutenant* Główczyński – 1 Messerschmitt – which fell south of Andelys
2) *Lieutenant* Czerniak – 1 Messerschmitt – which fell south of Andelys
3) section: *Cne* Wczelik, *Lieutenant* Kowalski and *Sergt* Markiewicz downed a Dornier aircraft, which fell on Louviers.
4) *Sergent* Parafiński – 1 Messerschmitt – which fell on Louviers.
Pilots who took part in combats:
Cdt Kępiński, *Cdt* Marmier, *Cne* Łaguna, *S/lieut.* Lachowicki, *Cap.Chef* Niewiara, *S/lieutenant* Zadroziński, *Sergent* Palak, *Cap.Chef* Uchto, *Lieutenant* Obuchowski, *S/lieutenant* Skibiński, *S/lieutenant* Godlewski
Forced landed: *Cdt* Kępiński, *Lieut.* Czerniak, *Lieut.* Skibiński, *Lieut.* Godlewski
No information from: *S/Lieut.* Lachowicki, *Cap-Chef* Uchto, *Lieut.* Obuchowski
Lieut. Kowalski is wounded in the right arm.
Addressed to:
Mr le Général Cdt de Groupement 21
Mr le Général Cdt de Groupement 42
Mr le Colonel Cdt de Groupement 23

Commanding GC 1/145
/–/
Kępiński *Maj.* pil

1 2,000 m – author's note

53

[53]: The 'Caudron Avenue' as seen from the Chartres–Dreux road. First right is the Miles Magister with its engine removed. (B. Belcarz coll.)

Messerschmitts remained with the bombers. The GC 1/145 report that summarised the combat, said:

Without a doubt, the engagement over Vernon was the biggest combat of GC 1/145 pilots during the entire French campaign. It was paid for by the loss of three pilots (Lt Jan Obuchowski, 2nd Lt Lech Lachowicki-Czechowicz, LAC Edward Uchto). These pilots were probably shot down by Lt. Josef Bürschgens (from the 7./JG26, at 15.15 near Mantes)[32], Lt. Heinz Ebeling (8./JG26, 15.30 near Rouen)[33] and Fw. Josef Gärtner (8./JG26, 15.35).[34]

Four aeroplanes landed damaged at airfields: three at Dreux (Maj. Józef Kępiński, Lt Jerzy Czerniak, 2nd Lt Bronisław Skibiński) and the fourth one, flown by 2nd Lt Jerzy Godlewski, at Villacoublay. Godlewski's Caudron had serious problems with the engine right from the take-off. When climbing, at about 4,500 m the engine lost power and Godlewski entered a dive, hoping that the engine might work better at a lower altitude. This happened at about 2,000 m, but he thus stayed far behind the GC 1/145 formation. Despite attempts he was unable to rejoin it. After climbing back to about 4,000 m, Godlewski lost visual contact with his squadron just as they started their attack on the German formation. A moment later he spotted a group which he identified as nine Heinkel He 111s. Before he could plan an attack, a section of German bombers, identified by Godlewski as Dornier Do 217s, appeared near his Caudron. The pilot forgot to unlock the guns at first. Realising his mistake, he then fired at the German bomber, noting hits on the starboard wing and the port engine. The aeroplane broke away from the formation, and Godlewski opened fire on another enemy machine. However, after a short burst the guns stopped firing due to lack of ammunition. Godlewski's aeroplane was also hit, but he managed to reach the Villacoublay airfield .

The next day Godlewski attempted to fly to Dreux in another aeroplane that he collected at Villacoublay. His attempt failed when the aeroplane hit a carelessly filled bomb crater and crashed during the take-off run. On 10 June, Godlewski informed about this incident by phone, talking to Capt. Łaguna, at the time the acting commander of the GC 1/145. In the confusion of the evacuation the pilot failed to rejoin the squadron and he was evacuated to Africa via Port Vendres together with Capt. Franciszek Fugiel.[35]

Lt Julian Kowalski, wounded in the arm, returned to Dreux from the combat on 9 June.

The operation has significantly reduced the number of GC 1/145 aircraft. Six CR.714s were completely destroyed, two more seriously damaged. Of the 17 aircraft used in the operation, eight were lost: nearly 50% of those involved. The inventory of the squadron was reduced dramatically.

According to French reports, the GC 1/145 attack on the German formation was successful for the Polish fighters. As mentioned in the report quoted earlier, four pilots of the squadron were credited with victories: three against Bf 109s and one against a Do 17. Analysis of available reports from the German side does not confirm this. The III./JG26 that operated

32 2,000 m – author's note

33 The CR.714 of *LAC* Uchto crashed at Villiers-en-Désoeuvre (dep. Eure 27), 35 km north of Dreux.

34 The CR.714 flown by 2nd Lt Lech Lachowicki-Czechowicz crashed at Normanville (dep. Seine-Maritime 76), 35 km east of Rouen.

35 O.K.L. C.2036/II Nr. 49737/40 film, Bundesarchiv, and J.Prien, G.Stemmer, P.Rodeike, W.Bock, *Jagdfliegerverbände der Deutschen Luftwaffe 1934 bis 1945, teil 3*. The German source did not indicate the location of the shoot-down. The last of the Caudrons lost that day by the GC 1/145 (Lt Obuchowski's) crashed at Normanville (dep. Eure 27) 5 km north of Evreux. Coincidentally, the crash locations of Obuchowski and Lachowicki-Czechowicz have the same name, but they are located in various departements, about 60 km away from one another.

[54]: *A German sentry guarding the wrecks at the Dreux airfield. The photo was taken from a car travelling from Dreux towards Chartres. (B. Belcarz coll.)*

[55]: *A diagram showing the repositioning of selected CR.714s at the Dreux airfield by the Germans.*

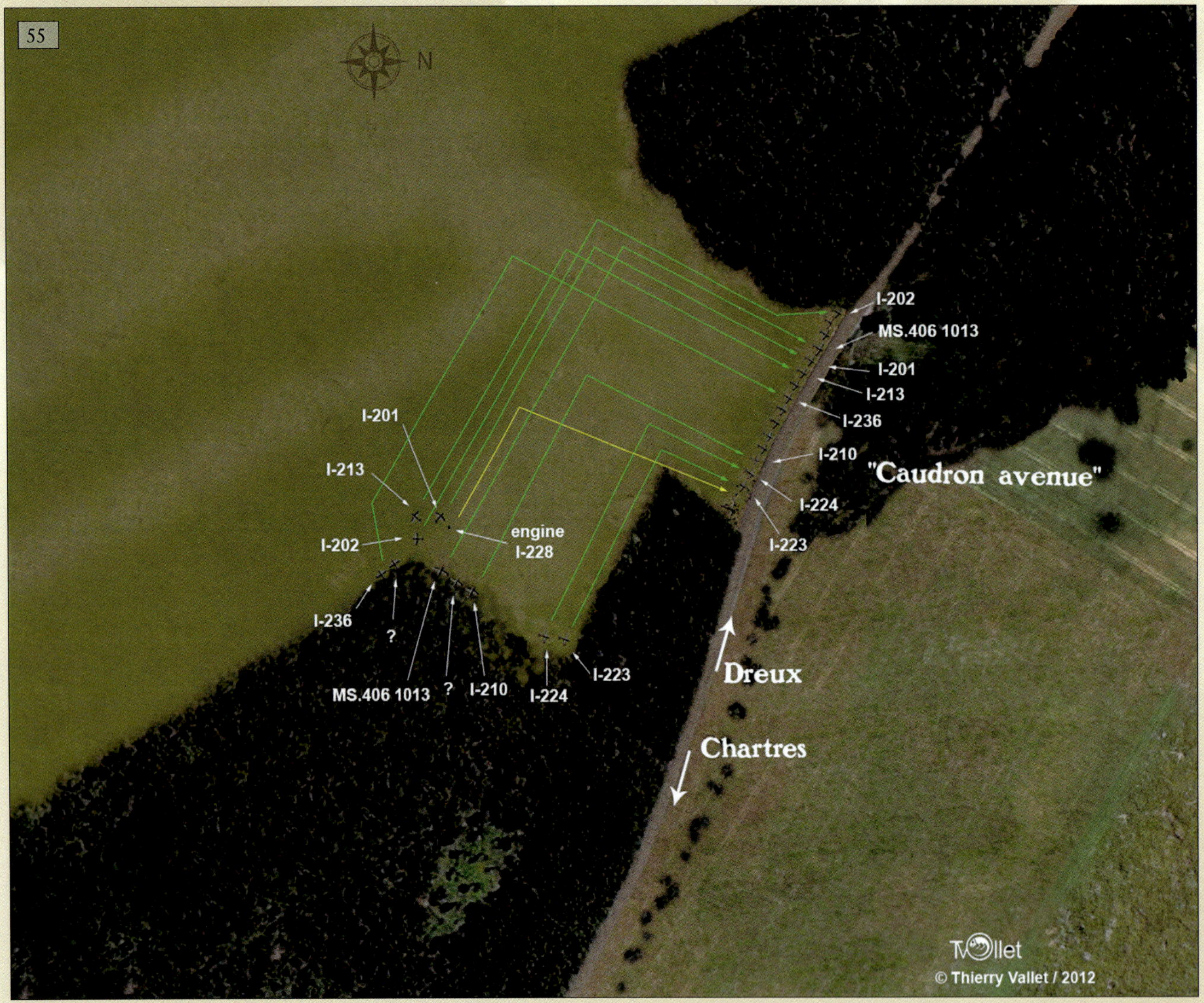

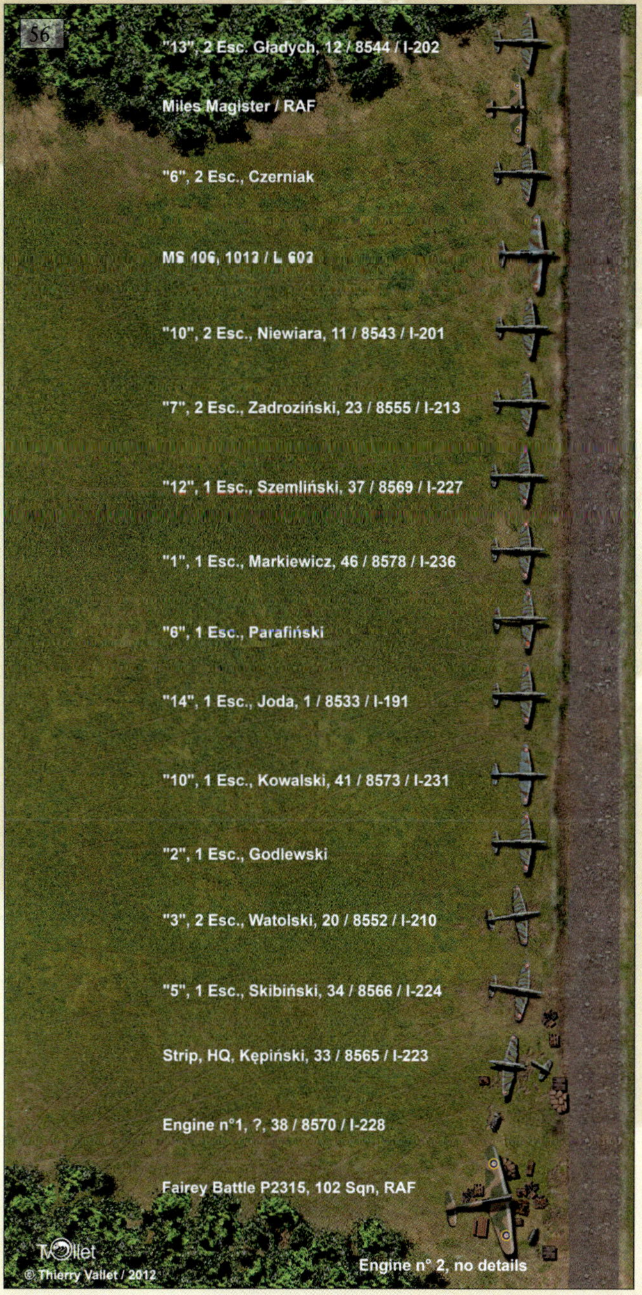

[56]: An exact diagram showing the location of aircraft at Dreux at the end of June 1940.

in the area suffered no combat losses since 8 June 1940. There is also no information about any KG2 Do 17 loss in the area.

Three light sections (nine CR.714s) returned from Berney in the evening. Also in the evening, a heavy section (five CR.714s) was scrambled, alerted by the warning network about approaching German aeroplanes. The Dreux railway station was their target. The information arrived late and the Polish aeroplanes stood no chance of intercepting the German bombers. The railway station was seriously damaged, and telephone communication was broken. The GC 1/145 section was airborne between 20.10 and 20.55.

The German air raids caused panic among the residents of Dreux, who began to leave the city en masse.

10 June

That day, the unit received information about NCO promotions with effect from 3 May 1940. A. Markiewicz, L. Szempliński, J. Palak and E. Paterek were promoted to the permanent rank of Sergeant, while P. Zaniewski, M. J. Parafiński and A. Niewiara to the rank of Corporal.

The unfavourable development of situation at the front line forced the French HQ to move some French air units towards Brittany. These orders also concerned the GC II/10 based at Berney, with which the GC 1/145 pilots had successfully cooperated in previous days. Thus, the Polish unit at Dreux became exposed to a direct German attack, and the airfield area could be threatened by enemy mechanised troops at any time.

At about 8.30 a radio signal (from the Eiffel Tower) was received at Dreux about an approaching German raid. The squadron was able to commit 13 serviceable CR.714s. The information arrived relatively late and GC 1/145 aeroplanes had to enter the combat on the terms of the Germans. The Polish formation was led by the squadron commander Maj. Kępiński (CR.714 c/n 8556, I-214). He was accompanied by Cdt de Marmier and Capt. Łaguna from the HQ section; Capt. Wczelik, 2nd Lt Łukaszewicz, 2nd Lt Żukowski and Cpl Joda from the 1 Esc.; and two sections from the 2 Esc.: Capt. Frey, 2nd Lt Czerniak, 2nd Lt Zadroziński and 2nd Lt Wróblewski, Cpl Paterek, LAC Niewiara. At about 3,500 m, the GC 1/145 pilots intercepted a raid of 15 Dornier Do 17s escorted by 12 Bf 109s from the JG3.

Maj. Kępiński gave the following account from this part of the mission:

"After breaking the clouds upwards, I suddenly see the Nazi group: two swarms of dots fly straight at us. The lower ones are probably bombers. They are covered from above by fighters. The latter zigzag, trying not to overtake their bomb-laden charges. [...] The Nazi formation is growing rapidly. Dornier Do-17s! [...] The head-on attack lasted a second, maybe two. I managed to give a short burst at the leading machine of the formation, and both groups passed at an enormous speed. I turned sharply to the port. I saw two smoking Dorniers. Tracer streaks next to my machine reminded me that German fighters would not allow any further firing on their bombers with impunity. I make a sharp turn, dive, turn in the other direction, and dive. Well, finally, I shook two fighters off my tail, [...] I'm aiming at a machine that fiercely attacks my deputy's Caudron. After a while, the situation is made clear. The German gave up the fight. [...] I am relieved to see a section of four from my squadron moving among the highly elevated cumulus. It appears for a moment, then hides in the cloud again. In order not to lose them, I put my Caudron nose down and aim at the place where they should soon emerge from the white-grey mist. [...] There they are! I instinctively throttle back... and

57

[57]: One of the earliest photos depicting Maj. Józef Kępiński's CR.714 c/n 8565 after the forced landing at Dreux on 9 June 1940. The wreck was camouflaged with branches. (B. Belcarz coll.)

at the same moment my heart is in my mouth. They weren't aeroplanes from my squadron, but Nazi Messerschmitts. I'm trying to fly away. Perhaps they didn't notice? Suddenly I felt as if someone had whipped my back. At the same time, an invisible hand smashed all the instruments in my cockpit to pieces. The burst was well aimed. I make a turn in the other direction and enter a dive. Left hand inert. I'm weaker and weaker every moment. There is no question of baling out. Landing is the only rescue. Will I have enough strength, will I make it? Black spots fly before my eyes. Ground! I feel the impact and darkness overwhelms me..."[36]

Kępiński managed to survive, heavily wounded, landing with his last effort at the Chartres airfield. The victory over Kępiński (at 8.35 French time)[37] is attributed to the 1./JG3 commander, Oblt. Lothar Keller. His second victim, two minutes later, was apparently the Caudron of 2nd Lt Łukaszewicz.[38]

Łukaszewicz noticed that Maj. Kępiński found himself in trouble and went to help his commander.[39] He then recalled:

"Immediately after take-off we saw them: twenty-four Dorniers[40] escorted by about fifteen Messerschmidts. They flew quite high, at four thousand meters. How slowly our Caudrons climbed! It seemed we would never get them.

"I admit that this was my first air combat against such a large formation, so when their fighters started attacking us from above, I felt very uncomfortable. [...] At one point [...] I saw a pair of ours, whom I tried to join. While approaching them I saw that they were attacked tail-on by two Germans, completely unnoticed. I did not manage to warn them, I just saw a burst fired from a very close distance and the aeroplane of the squadron commander, which I recognised by the markings on the tail[41], falling into a spin. I was so close that after making a violent turn I found myself behind the same Jerry who had downed my boss. I fired until he went down in flames.[42] However, [...] another one came to his aid by getting on my tail. I think he would have killed me had my engine not caught fire. Seeing the tracers criss-crossing around me, I thought at that moment that I had been hit, so I opened the canopy and prepared to bale out, but the fire went out by itself, while the German, sure that I was burning, left me alone. Seeing that the situation was not dangerous, I glided to the Garennes-sur-Eure airfield (about 18 km north of Dreux) and landed, trailing smoke all the time."[43]

36 Letter from EMAA no. 2427 1/1S of 19 June 1940.

37 An account from the family archive also quoted in: T. Malinowski, *Polskie skrzydła nad Francją 1940 rok* pp. 13–15

38 There was an hour's difference between the French and German time.

39 J. Prien, G. Stemmer, P.Rodeike, W.Bock, *Die Jagdfliegerverbande der Deutschen Luftwaffe 1934 bis 1945. Teil 3 Einsatz in Danemark und Norwegen 9.4. bis 30.11.1940. Der Feldzug im Westen 10.5. bis 25.6.1940*, p. 156.

40 This is probable. The account filed by .2nd Lt Łukaszewicz on 28 October 1941 supports this. Even though it includes some inaccuracies, it generally confirms the course of the action.

41 Other pilots reported a smaller number of Dorniers.

42 Kępiński's personal machine (c/n 8565, I-223) had been seriously damaged the previous day and was lying, unserviceable (damaged undercarriage) at the Dreux airfield. Perhaps Łukaszewicz meant the code number, as the pilots were probably notified before taking off about the markings of the squadron commander's Caudron during that mission.

43 This fact cannot be corroborated. However, if Łukaszewicz attacked the aeroplane of Oblt. Lothar Keller, then the latter could not have scored a double victory, and

Meanwhile, other Polish aeroplanes attacked the German bombers, while the Messerschmitts of the escort came to the latter's aid. There was a series of individual dog-fights. 2nd Lt Czerniak, whose take-off had been delayed compared to the other aeroplanes of the squadron, reported shooting down a Do 17 of the section that closed the bomber formation, over Dreux.[44] Another German bomber was claimed shot down by 2nd Lt Żukowski.[45] Moments later both of them had to take evasive action from the escorting Bf 109s. Cpl Paterek (attacked two Do 17s, had to abandon the attack because of two intervening Bf 109s), Lt Zadroziński and 2nd Lt Wróblewski all reported inconclusive engagements with German aeroplanes. Capt. Łaguna claimed a probable victory over a Bf 109, which he apparently chased as far as northern Paris.[46]

Soon after returning from the morning mission came an opportunity for another clash with the Germans. About 10.40 twelve Caudrons were scrambled. The take-off was in connection with information received from the sector HQ about approaching enemy aeroplanes coming from the direction of Vernon towards Dreux. The Polish formation was as follows: Col. Pawlikowski (from the HQ section), 1 Esc. pilots: Capt. Wczelik, Lt Kowalski, Lt Czerwiński, Cpl Parafiński and 2 Esc. pilots: Capt. Frey, Lt Wilczewski, 2nd Lt Czerniak, 2nd Lt Główczyński, 2nd Lt Jaugsch, Sgt Palak and LAC Zieliński. The pilots initially encountered no enemy in the designated sector. After a while, as described in the unit's report by Capt. Łaguna: "One of our sections spotted an aeroplane over the area and dived to identify it. That aeroplane started firing and ours as well. The aeroplane was diving and at that moment we recognised that it was English."[47]

This brief note does not specify which of the GC 1/145 pilots opened fire on the Battle from No. 103 Squadron RAF and what the effect of this engagement was. The situation is complicated because it is difficult to clearly identify the cause of the loss of Fairey Battle no. P2328 (P/O Thomas and LAC Bligh).[48] According to the entries in the Operations Record Book of the squadron, it can be concluded that the unit lost one Battle during its attack on German river crossings, while two more suffered damage.[49] The aeroplane piloted by F/O Kelly was fired upon by friendly fighters (the British document specified a Hawker Hurricane, but in fact that was probably the Polish Caudron), while another (piloted by Sgt Critch) was damaged by anti-aircraft artillery fire. The report of Capt. Łaguna specifies that the target of the identification (attack) of the GC 1/145 CR.714 was a single British aeroplane, so it can be guessed that it was the Battle flown by F/O Kelly. Therefore, linking the loss of Battle P2328 with the GC 1/145 Caudron attack may be wrong, and this Battle may have been a victim of the anti-aircraft fire, just like that of Sgt Critch.

10 June was the last day of GC 1/145 operations from Dreux. According to the report of Capt. Łaguna, the combat effort of the GC 1/145 during its stay at Dreux totalled 19 operational missions with a total time of 188 flying hours.

the shooting down of Łukaszewicz would have to be credited to an unknown pilot of the JG3.

44 The account of 2nd Lt M. Łukaszewicz in the author's collection, courtesy of Z. Charytoniuk.

45 German sources do not confirm any loss of a Do 17 from a bomber unit in that area. The only Do 17 lost there belonged to a reconnaissance unit, the 2.(F)/11, and crashed at Boullay-les-Troux (about 35 km east of Dreux, the crew of Oblt. Klaus Stecher, Fw. Heinz Sehlmacher, Fw. Joseph Hermann were all killed). The aeroplane performed reconnaissance on the route of Rambouilliet – Blois – Nevers – Montargis, having taken off at 5.30.

46 Łukaszewicz also claimed that victory in his report of 10 June. In view of the above account it is hard to assume that he participated in that unconfirmed victory. Even more so, as the listing made by P. Łaguna on 13 June 1940 does no include the name of Łukaszewicz.

47 J. Prien, G. Stemmer, P.Rodeike, W.Bock, *Die Jagdfliegerverbande der Deutschen Luftwaffe 1934 bis 1945. Teil 3 Einsatz in Danemark und Norwegen 9.4. bis 30.11.1940. Der Feldzug im Westen 10.5. bis 25.6.1940*, p. 165. The only loss of the JG3 that day was a Messerschmitt 109 E-3 seriously damaged (70%) in air combat over Vernon, which belonged to the II./JG3 (pilot unknown), which was then struck off charge. *Capt*. P. Łaguna was probably the victor.

48 *Compte rendu special du 9.VI.40 – 10.VI. du midi* (Special report from 9 June to midday 10 June).

49 W. R. Chorley, *Bomber Command losses of the Second World War 1939–1940*, p.75. Battle P2328 crashed at Gasny (Eure) 8 km south-east of Vernon.

Evacuation from Dreux

11 June

The evacuation of French air units based in the area on the previous day and the development of the fighting on 10 June caused concern in the GC 1/145. This was further supported by the premature information, which reached Dreux on 11 June, about a German motorised unit advancing from Louviers.[50] The prevailing mood in the squadron is shown by the forming of an anti-paratroop squad, whose soldiers were to sleep with their weapons, and in the event of an alert they had to leave immediately to places indicated by the duty officer. The officer quartered in a bus. Instructions for the anti-aircraft section were also tightened.[51]

Since the wounded squadron commander was hospitalised, command of the unit was taken by Capt. Piotr Łaguna. The vacant post of the deputy squadron commander was taken

50 *Lt Col* Salesse (ed.): *L'aviation polonaise en France 1939–40*, p. 252bis.

51 1/145 Fighter Squadron. Daily orders no. 22 of 11 June 1940.

[58–60[: After removing the camouflaging, the wreck aroused interest among German soldiers. This brought a devastating effect in a relatively short time. Photos [58] and [59] also show the wreck of CR.714 c/n 8566 (I-224) code no. 5 from the 1 Esc., assigned to 2nd Lt Skibiński. (B. Belcarz coll.)

over by the 1 Esc. commander, Capt. Antoni Wczelik, while his duties were taken over by Lt Tadeusz Czerwiński.

A decision of the HQ ordered an immediate move to Sermaises, about 15 km south of Etampes (in fact to the Césarville and Janville airfield hub).

Thirteen CR.714s were airworthy. Fifteen aircraft were left at the airfield.[52] Moreover, Morane Saulnier MS.406 c/n 1013[53] and two British aircraft: Fairey Battle I no. P2315[54] and a Miles Magister[55] were also left at Dreux.

An exact diagram showing the location of aircraft at Dreux (at the end of June 1940) is shown beside.

Capt. Łaguna noted in his report:

According to the order of Cdt Marmier, with whom I was leaving the Dreux airfield with 15 mechanics, I have not burnt the abandoned equipment.[56]

All the parts that could be used to repair the remaining machines of the squadron were cannibalised from the abandoned aircraft. Machine guns and ammunition were also removed. This duty was carried out by soldiers of the Compagnie de l'Air 46/104 over two subsequent days. In addition, they ploughed through the landing field making it difficult for the Germans to use it.

The evacuated aeroplanes flew to Janville. One of these was damaged during landing. This is described by G/C Roger Teillet, a pilot of the GC I/1, in his memoirs:

A few Caudron 714 aeroplanes attempt to land at Janville. One of theses damages the undercarriage at the edge of the runway.[57]

From that day, the GC 1/145 had no radio station, which practically limited any possibility of an operational employment of the unit.

52 M. Comas, *Les chasseurs Caudron*, mentions on p. 60 about 16 aircraft abandoned at Dreux. But the listing of equipment left in France attached to the report of Capt. Łaguna lists 15 aircraft, including 11 repairable and 4 crashed in landings. Detailed analysis of available photographic material makes me inclined to agree with Łaguna.

53 According to *Lt Col* Salesse (ed.): *L'aviation polonaise en France 1939–40*, p. 253 the Morane belonged to an unspecified French unit and its presence at Dreux was due to a forced landing.

54 The aeroplane from 103 Squadron RAF (crew: P/O G.W.Thorougood, Sgt Asson, P/O Webber) was forced to land on 8 June 1940 following a sortie over Poix.

55 From an unidentified unit.

56 P. Łaguna, *Sprawozdanie bojowe z działalności Dyonu za czas od 10.V.40 do 19.VI.40.*

57 M. Comas, *Les chasseurs Caudron*, p. 60.

The aircraft lost during operations from the Dreux airfield

Several aeroplanes were lost during operations from the Dreux airfield. Three of these were lost irretrievably in air combat. The following pilots were killed: 2nd Lt Lech Lachowicki-Czechowicz (code no. 14 – 2 Esc?), Lt Jan Obuchowski (no. 4 – 1 Esc?), LAC Edward Uchto (no. 8 – 2 Esc?). For a long time, it seemed that it would prove impossible to unearth photographs documenting these losses. This was due to the fact that wreckage of the wooden Caudron that had hit the ground in uncontrolled flight would probably be extremely difficult to identify.

Subsequent aircraft were abandoned at various airfields, mainly for technical reasons. C/n 8549 (I-207) ended up at the Evreux airfield. This aircraft was damaged during air combat on 8 June 1940, when flown by 2nd Lt Aleksy Żukowski. He landed at Evreux with Capt. Wczelik and Cpl Zaniewski. The next day, Wczelik and Zaniewski returned to Dreux, while the unserviceable no. 13 remained at Evreux, where it was then captured by the Germans. This aeroplane is known from photographs taken by KG53 staff.

The Caudron flown by 2nd Lt Jerzy Godlewski landed at the Villacoublay airfield following a combat on 9 June 1940. Information about the serial or code number of the aircraft flown by Godlewski on that occasion is not available. It may have been c/n 8587, I-245 shown in photos in the Villacoublay chapter (although this remains unconfirmed). It is known, however, that he collected another machine at the factory, in which he crashed while taking off.

Another Caudron, the identification of which causes no problem, is c/n 8556 (I-214). The aeroplane was flown by Maj. Józef Kępiński, the commander of the squadron, during his last sortie. He was seriously wounded and landed at the Chartres airfield. The aeroplane was captured by the Germans after they occupied the city. Nominally, this aeroplane was usually flown by Cpl Paterek. However, on 9 June 1940 it was the squadron commander who used it, as he had damaged his personal machine (c/n 8565, I-223) the previous day at Dreux.

The Caudron of Lt Łukaszewicz (c/n 8550, I-208) was another aeroplane that took off from that airfield but failed to return there. The only certain information is that he made a forced landing near an airfield (Garenne?). The pilot returned to his unit, and photos of the aircraft were published in the German magazine Deutsche Luftwacht. Ausgabe Luftwissen Bd. 7 in July 1940. It was an aeroplane of the *1 Escadrille* with a small white code no. 11 on the fin.

61

62

[61–64]: Caudron-Renault CR.714 c/n 8565 (under-wing no. I-223), pilot – Maj. Józef Kępiński GC 1/145. Dreux, June 1940.

63

64

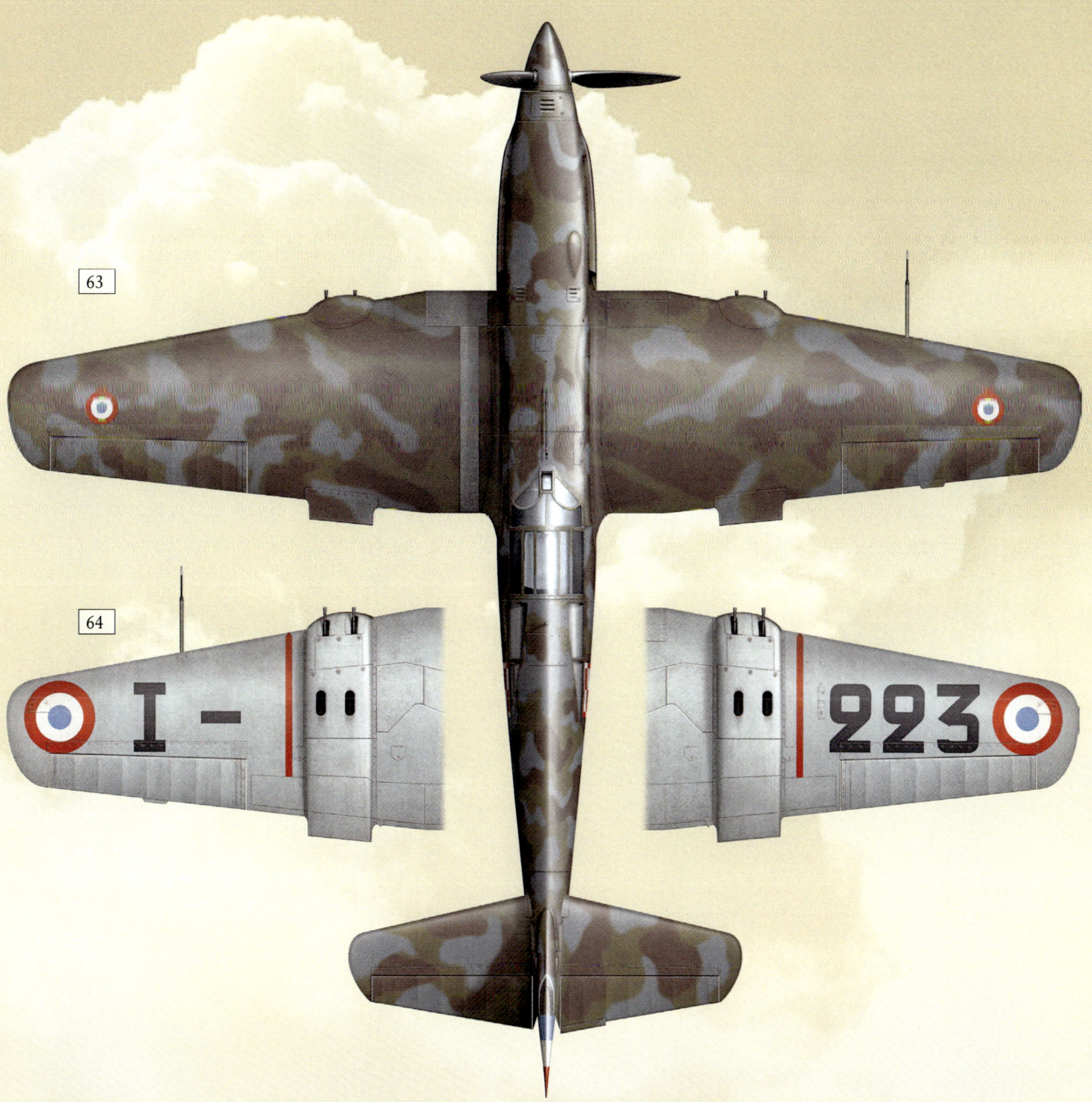

65

[65]: The wreck of CR.714 c/n 8565 (I-223). The propeller spinner of CR.714 c/n 8566 (I-224) can be seen beneath the port wing. (B. Belcarz coll.)

66

67

[66–69]: Caudron-Renault CR.714 c/n 8543, code no. 10 (under-wing no. I-201), pilot – LAC Andrzej Niewiara, 2 Esc. GC 1/145. Dreux, June 1940.

68

69

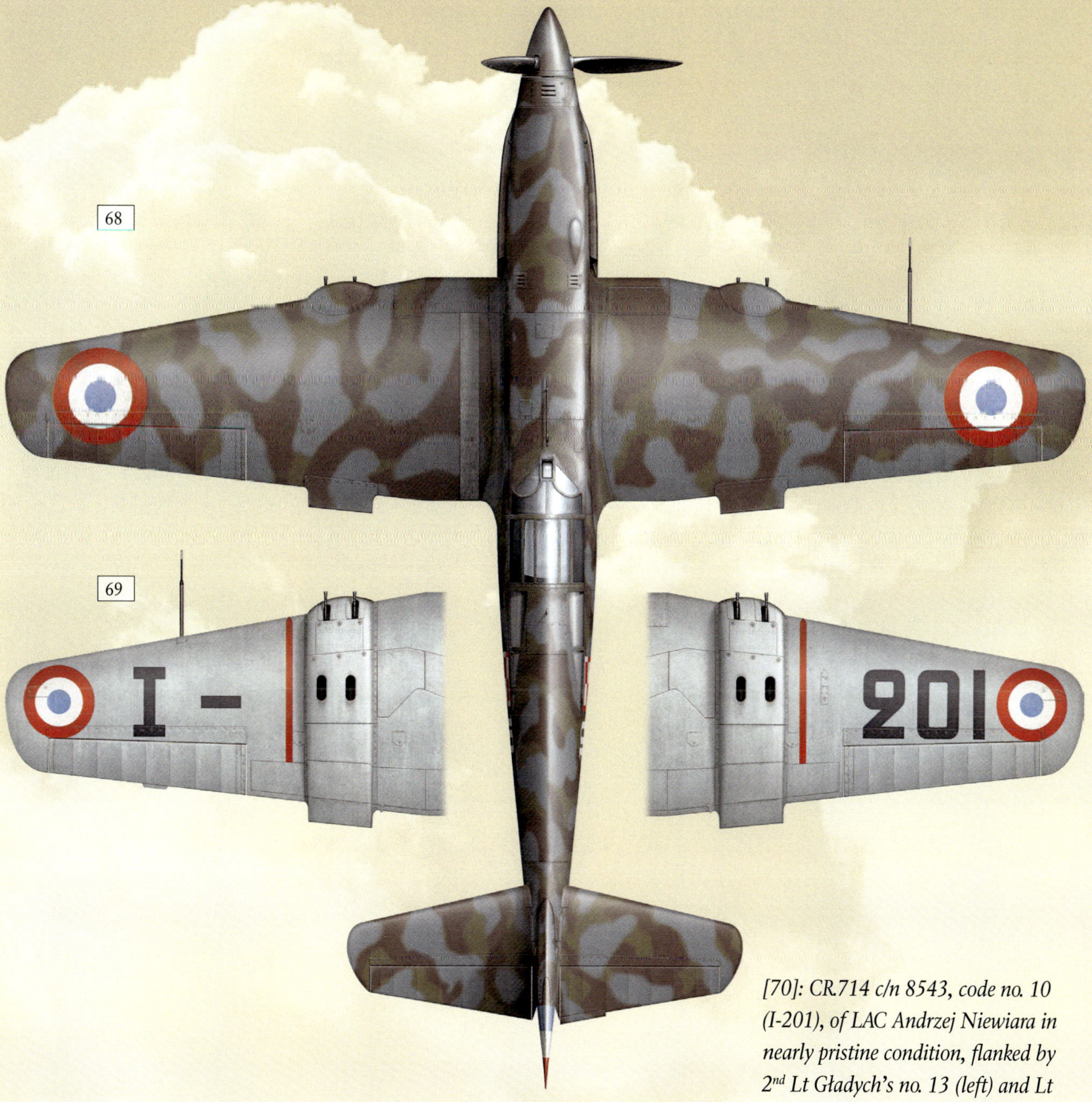

[70]: CR.714 c/n 8543, code no. 10 (I-201), of LAC Andrzej Niewiara in nearly pristine condition, flanked by 2nd Lt Gładych's no. 13 (left) and Lt Zadroziński's no. 7 s. (B. Belcarz coll.)

70

71

[71]: *Rear view of LAC Niewiara's CR.714. The aircraft still displays full markings on the fuselage (Ph. Ricco coll.)*

[72]: *The Polish national markings were the first 'souvenirs' removed from the aircraft. GC 1/145 aircraft were usually carefully camouflaged with tree branches, which suggests that the group of aircraft shown in this sequence had been rearranged for German propaganda photos. (M. Comas coll.)*

72

73

[73, 74]: Two of the chronologically latest photos of Niewiara's no. 10. It should be noted that although vandalised since the first days, no. 10 has survived until the end in a much better condition than other aeroplanes of the squadron. (B. Belcarz coll.)

74

[75, 77]: Caudron-Renault CR.714 c/n 8544, code no. 13 (under-wing no. I-202), pilot – 2nd Lt Bolesław Gładych, 2 Esc. GC 1/145. Dreux, June 1940.

75

[76, 78]: 2nd Lt Bolesław Gładych was one of the best Polish pilots of the World War II. He commenced his combat career in France with the GC 1/145, posted to the 2 Escadrille under Capt. Frey. His personal CR.714, c/n 8544 (I-202), displayed white code no. 13 on the fuselage. The engine of CR.714 c/n 8570 (I-228) can be seen in the foreground of photo [76]. (B. Belcarz coll.)

76

77

78

79

80

[79–82]: Caudron-Renault CR.714 c/n 8555, code no. 7 (under-wing no. I-213), pilot – Lt Zdzisław Zadroziński, 2 Esc. GC 1/145. Dreux, June 1940.

81

82

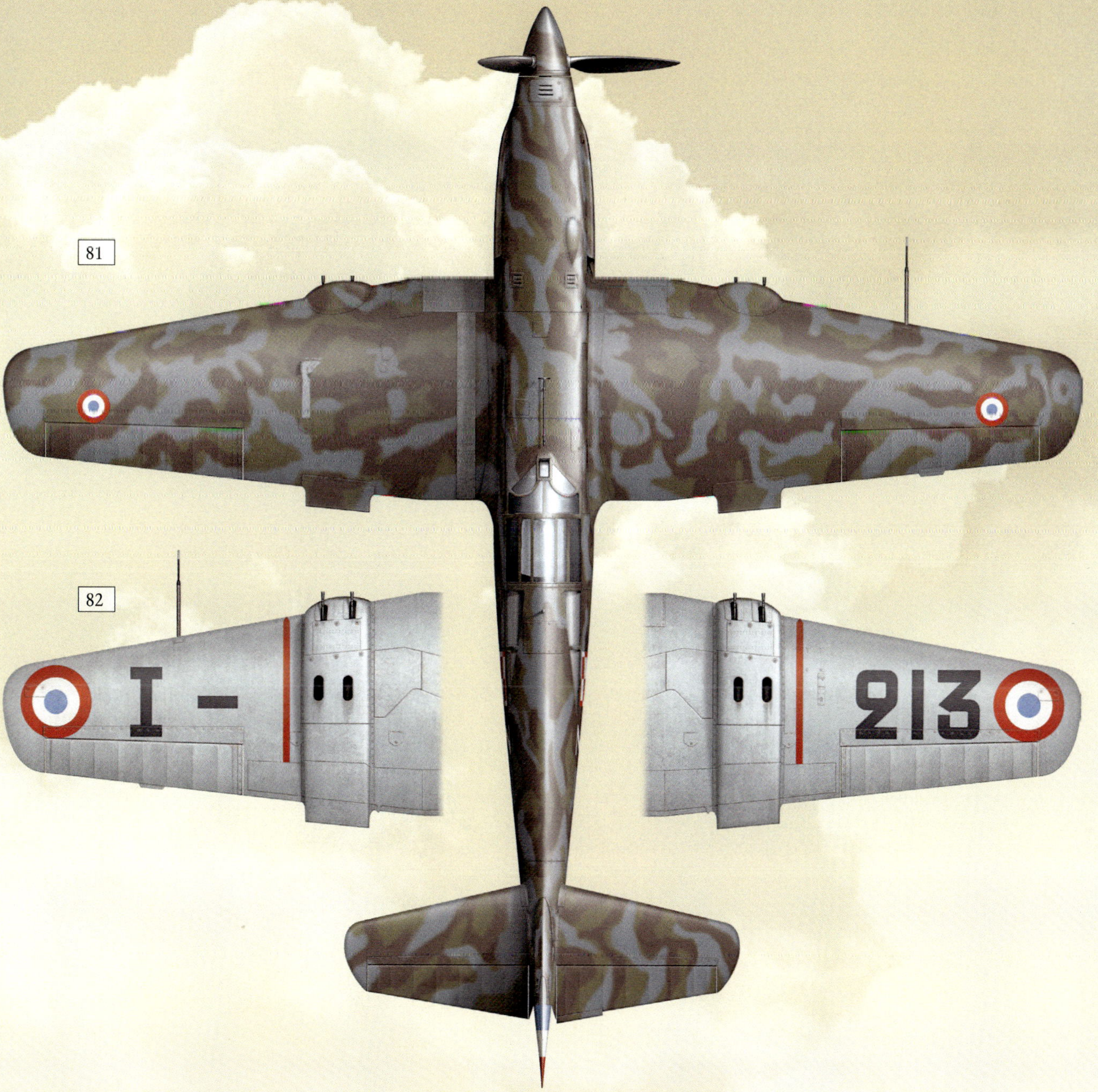

[83]: *Lt Zadroziński's aircraft can be seen in the background, showing clearly the old-style small roundels. 2nd Lt Gładych's aeroplane (with the vertical tail damaged by fire) is on the left (larger size French roundels applied on the upper wing surface). The rear fuselage of LAC Niewiara's aircraft is at right. (B. Belcarz coll.)*

83

84

85

86

[84-86]: Lt Zadroziński's CR.714 c/n 8555 (I-213) code no. 7 with two other aircraft of the 2 Esc. These are some of the earliest photographs taken by the Germans after they captured the Dreux airfield. The aircraft still displays the Polish national markings, soon removed by 'souvenir hunters'. (B. Belcarz coll., J. Crow)

87

[87, 88]: The central fuselage of Zadroziński's no. 7 in the foreground. The retractable radio mast is shown to advantage. Note the huge airfield fuel tank, probably German, visible in the background at right. The bottom photo reveals a panorama of 1 Esc. aircraft fins. The bottom photo also shows details of the aluminium sheet walkway that facilitated entering the cockpit and maintenance of the engine and the instruments. (B. Belcarz coll.)

88

[89, 91]: Caudron-Renault CR.714 c/n 8552, code no. 3 (under-wing no. I-210), pilot – LAC Ernest Watolski, 2 Esc. GC 1/145. Dreux, June 1940.

89

90

[90]: LAC Watolski's Caudron, c/n 8552 (I-210), photographed while the KG53 and KGrzbV1 were based at Dreux. 2nd Lt Skibiński's CR.714 c/n 8566 (I-224) from the 1 Esc., with a small code no. 5 on the tail, can be seen behind LAC Watolski's aeroplane. (B. Belcarz coll.)

51

92

[92]: LAC Watolski's Caudron at the time when the wrecks were successively removed from the airfield by the Germans. (B. Belcarz coll.)

[93]: Caudron-Renault CR.714 c/n 85?? (under-wing no. I-2??), pilot – 2nd Lt Jerzy Czerniak, 2 Esc. GC 1/145. Dreux, June 1940.

[94]: The first and so far the only known photo of the port side of code no. 6 from the 2 Esc. before the code marking was cut out. The photo shows the aeroplane in a relatively good condition, camouflaged on the edge of the copse near the Dreux airfield. (B. Belcarz coll.)

95

[95]: The photo shows a fragment of the starboard side of Czerniak's aeroplane. This proves that the code number on the port side had been cut out earlier than its equivalent here. (B. Belcarz coll.)

[96]: The port side, with the code number already removed, is known from several other photos. Unfortunately, there are no clear photos that would allow identification of the aircraft's serial and construction numbers. (B. Belcarz coll.)

96

97

98

[97–100]: *Caudron-Renault CR.714 c/n 8566, code no. 5 (under-wing no. I-224), pilot – 2nd Lt Bronisław Skibiński, 1 Esc. GC 1/145. Dreux, June 1940.*

99

100

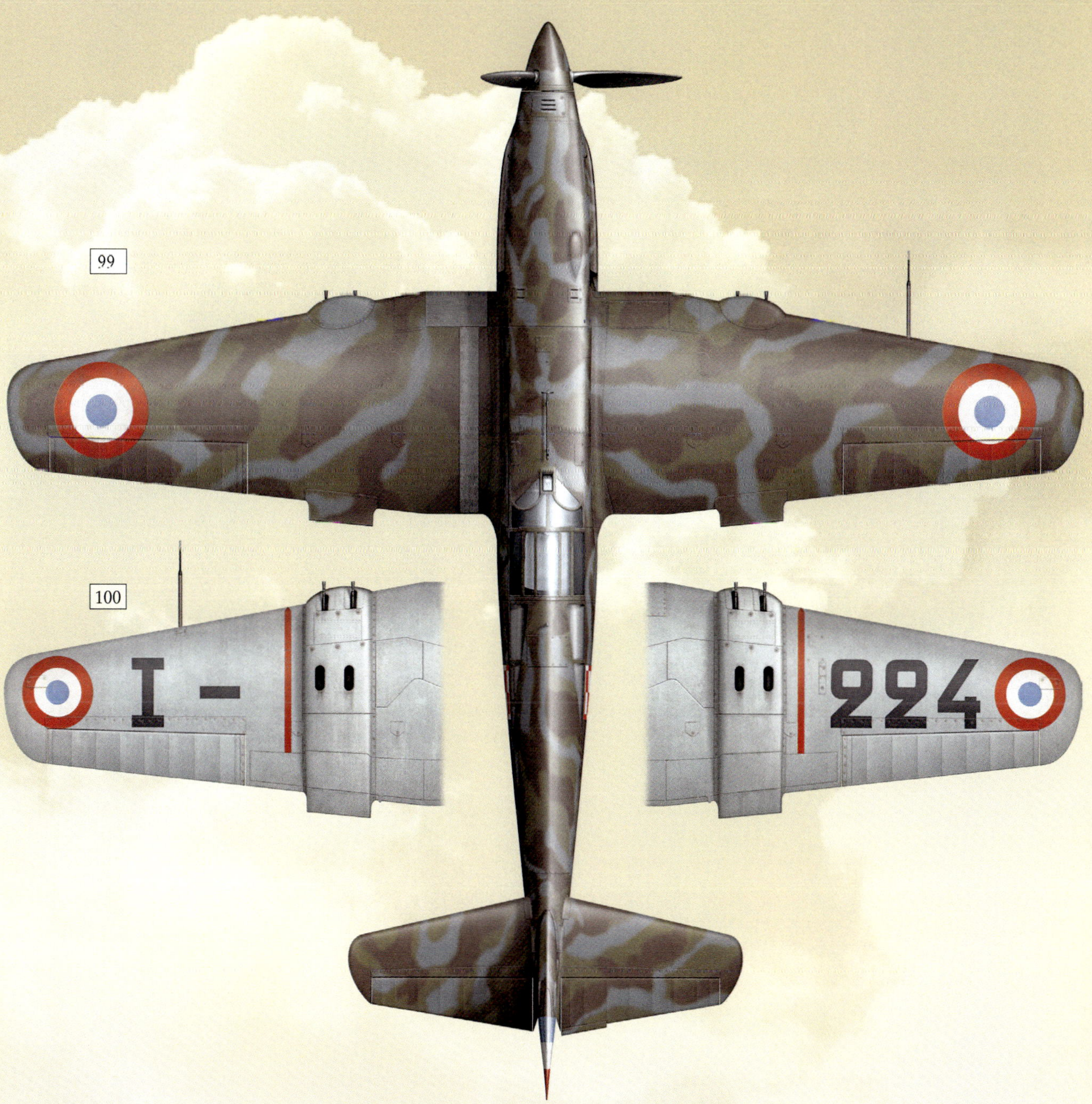

101

[101]: Damaged CR.714 c/n 8566, code no. 5 (I-244) of the 1 Esc. The camouflage pattern is shown clearly. The wreck of Maj. Kępiński's Caudron can be seen in the background. (G. Zaleski coll.)

102

[102, 103]: Some of the early photographs taken by the Germans at Dreux airfield on 15 June 1940. The aeroplane of 2nd Lt Bolesław Skibiński was often photographed together with the Caudron of Maj. Kępiński, as both these aeroplanes had landed at Dreux with damaged undercarriage and were subsequently moved to the part of the airfield where they were not an obstacle, and could be easily camouflaged with tree branches near the copse. (B. Belcarz coll.)

103

104

[104, 105]: Two photos of code no. 5 in the hands of the captors. Photo [105] shows colour division lines quite clearly. The two photos are a perfect illustration of how the quality of a photograph affects the appearance of the code number stroke width. In photo [104], less sharp, the white digit on dark background seems much thicker than in the lower one, the latter offering a much more accurate rendition of the reality. (B. Belcarz coll.)

105

106

[106, 108]: Caudron-Renault CR.714 c/n unknown,code no. 6, pilot – LAC Mieczysław Parafiński, 1 Esc. GC 1/145. Dreux, June 1940.

107

[107]: LAC Parafiński's aeroplane in June, in the 'Caudron Avenue'. The starboard engine cowling bent outwards was its characteristic feature. (J. Crow coll.)

108

[109]: *The Dreux 'catcher in the rye', as it appeared in a series of photos taken probably in late July or early August. (B. Belcarz coll.)*

109

[110]: Caudron-Renault CR.714 c/n 8578, code no. 1 (under-wing no. I-236), pilot – Cpl Antoni Markiewicz, 1 Esc. GC 1/145. Dreux, June 1940.

110

[111]: The group of Caudrons along the road to Dreux. Cpl Szempliński's code no. 12 (I-247) is in the foreground, with Cpl Markiewicz's aeroplane to its right – this is one of the best photos of the latter. (B. Belcarz coll.)

111

[112]: *Caudron-Renault CR.714 C/n unknown, code no. 2, pilot – 2nd Lt Jerzy Godlewski, 1 Esc. GC 1/145. Dreux, June 1940.*

112

113

[113]: *'Caudron Avenue'. 2nd Lt Jerzy Godlewski's CR.714 code no. 2 is in the foreground. The spine fairing of code no. 14 (I-191) from the 1 Esc. can be seen near its wing. C/n 8552, code no. 3 (I-210) from the 2 Esc., 8566 (I-224), code no. 5 of the 1 Esc. and Fairey Battle P2315 from No. 103 Sqn RAF can be seen behind it.*

[114]: Caudron-Renault CR.714 c/n 8573, code no. 10 (under-wing no. I-231), pilot – Lt Julian Kowalski, 1 Esc. GC 1/145. Dreux, June 1940.

114

115

116

[115, 116]: Lt Kowalski's 8573, code no. 10 (I-231) had several characteristic features: the almost uniform camouflage tone, the damage to the skin on its starboard side just aft of the cockpit, and the bright part of the fuselage framing visible after the Polish marking was cut out (at the rear edge of the cut-out). The port wing tip of Lt Godlewski's code no. 2 with parts of a large roundel can be seen in the foreground of photo [115]. (B. Belcarz coll.)

117

118

[117]: Probably the last photo of 1 Esc.'s no. 10, c/n 8573 (I-231) before it was taken away by the Germans from Dreux. A Renault engine from an unknown CR.714 is in the foreground. Unlike other machines, vandalised without mercy, no. 10 remained almost untouched until its last moments. (B. Belcarz coll.)

[118]: Details of the tail of c/n 8573. The tail of c/n 8533, code no. 14 (I-191) of the 1 Esc. can be seen behind it.

[119, 121]: Caudron-Renault CR.714 c/n 8589 (under-wing no. I-247), pilot – Cpl Lucjan Szempliński (Cdt Alexandre Lionel de Marmier), 1 Esc. GC 1/145. Dreux, June 1940.

119

120

[120]: According to squadron records c/n 8589 was initially the aeroplane of Cpl Szempliński, then it is listed as de Marmier's mount. It is probable that Szempliński's aeroplane was assigned to the Frenchman when the latter was posted into the GC 1/145 in June. (B. Belcarz coll.)

121

122

[122]: Cpl Lucjan Szempliński's Caudron has survived until the autumn of 1940 in a relatively good condition. All the French markings have been overpainted on it. Only the code number on the fin was left. (B. Belcarz coll.)

123

[123, 126]: *Caudron-Renault CR.714 c/n 8533 (under-wing no. I-191), pilot – LAC Antoni Joda, 1 Esc. GC 1/145. Dreux, June 1940.*

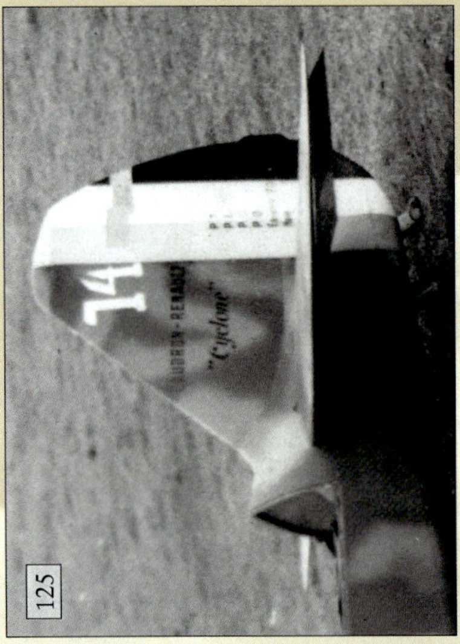

125

124

[124, 125]: *CR.714 c/n 8533 while still in the 'Caudron Avenue'.*

125

127

[127]: *As time passed, the aeroplane was vandalised. In this photo (taken by Graf zu Mürster), a German cross is visible on the port wing. German markings were applied on the Caudrons that were still at Dreux in the summer of 1940.*

Sermaises

12–13 June

The ground staff reached Sermaises on 12 June and was accommodated in an abandoned sugar factory. Sermaises and Janville belonged to the same airfield hub, located near Etampes. The move to Sermaises resulted in the transfer to the command of the Groupement de Chasse no. 23.

The GC 1/145 ground party reached the airfield in the evening. The unit remained at the Sermaisses airfield until the evening of 13 June. During this time, two operations were flown over enemy-held territory in a total flying time of about 6 hours. Out of the 12 aircraft that had left Dreux, 11 remained.

The earlier orders of General Astier de La Vigerie, responsible for the ZOAN, were put into effect on 12 June. According to letter No. 2144-S/3-0 of 12 June 1940, two groups were detached from the GC 1/145, to be sent for training in the GC I/1 and the GC I/8. The group sent to GC I/1 on 12 June, commanded by Capt. Wczelik, included the following pilots: 2nd Lt Bronisław Skibiński, 2nd Lt Aleksy Żukowski, Sgt Antoni Markiewicz, Sgt Lucjan Szempliński, Cpl Mieczysław Parafiński, Cpl Piotr Zaniewski and LAC Antoni Joda. The other group, commanded by Capt. Juliusz Frey, included: Lt Wacław Wilczewski, Lt Zdzisław Zadroziński, 2nd Lt Leon Jaugsch, 2nd Lt Czesław

[128]: For several dozen years after the war, no photo of a GC 1/145 CR.714 lost over the front line during the air combat in the afternoon of 9 June 1940 was known. Maj. Kępiński reached the Dreux airfield and little was known about the other pilots. Although the places where they were shot down were identified, other details were unknown. The photo is unique because it shows the remains of the CR.714 of 2nd Lt Lech Lachowicki-Czechowicz. His aeroplane crashed at Normanville (Departement Seine-Maritime 76, between Rouen and Amiens) and the pilot was killed. He lost his engagement with Lt. Heinz Ebeling from 8./JG26 about 15.30 in the Rouen area. Analysis of the remains of his aircraft suggests that the pilot tried to belly-land, probably in a burning aeroplane. This is evidenced by the propeller blades bent during landing with the undercarriage up. Other aircraft, burnt by the Germans at airfields (at Dreux, for example) had undamaged propeller blades. This aeroplane landed relatively successfully (the burnt remains are located together) and then it was probably destroyed by fire. The Caudron, as an all-wooden design, was prone to fire. The photo shows the engine with the propeller, ammunition magazines with machine gun barrels and the armoured plate that protected the back of the pilot. The machine could be identified thanks to the description on the back of the print: "Gut getroffen [well hit] Montdidier". This town is to the south of Amiens. Montdidier was one of the major places before Normanville en route to Rouen (the probable route of the photographer). Lt. Heinz Ebeling was an ace who scored 18 'kills' by the time he was shot down on 5 November 1940. He spent the rest of the war in English captivity. (B. Belcarz coll.)

128

129

130

[129–131]: This is undoubtedly the best-documented aeroplane of the GC 1/145. According to the report of Łaguna, c/n 8549 (I-207) landed at Evreux because it was hit in the engine by German bullets. The aeroplane at the Evreux airfield was almost complete and still had the Polish national markings on both sides of the fuselage. The aircraft featured the early undercarriage, but with no pressure in the shock absorbers it looked similar to the late one. (B. Belcarz coll., Ph. Couderchon coll.)

131

132

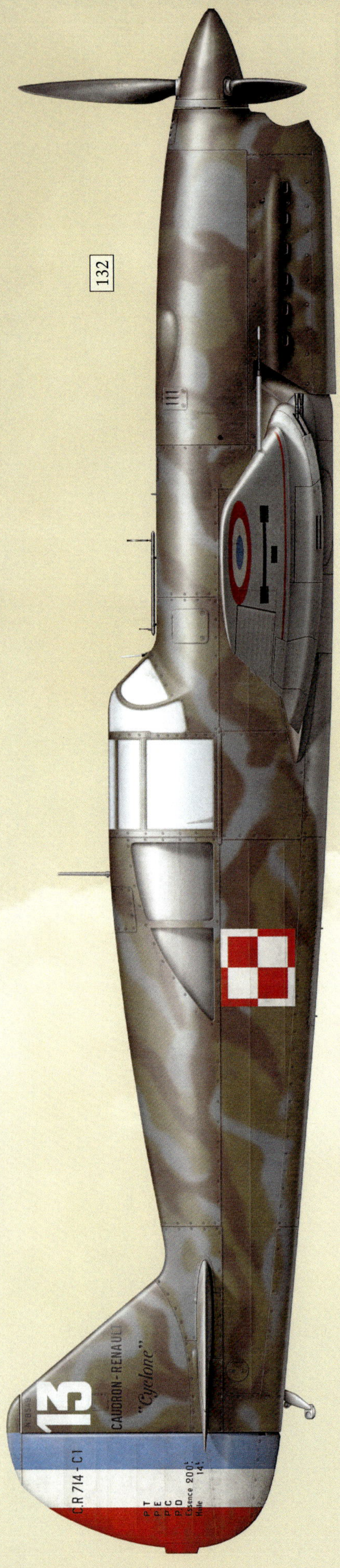

[132–135]: *Caudron-Renault CR.714 c/n 8549 (under-wing no. I-207), pilot – 2nd Lt Aleksy Żukowski, 1 Esc. GC 1/145. Evreux, June 1940.*

133

134

135

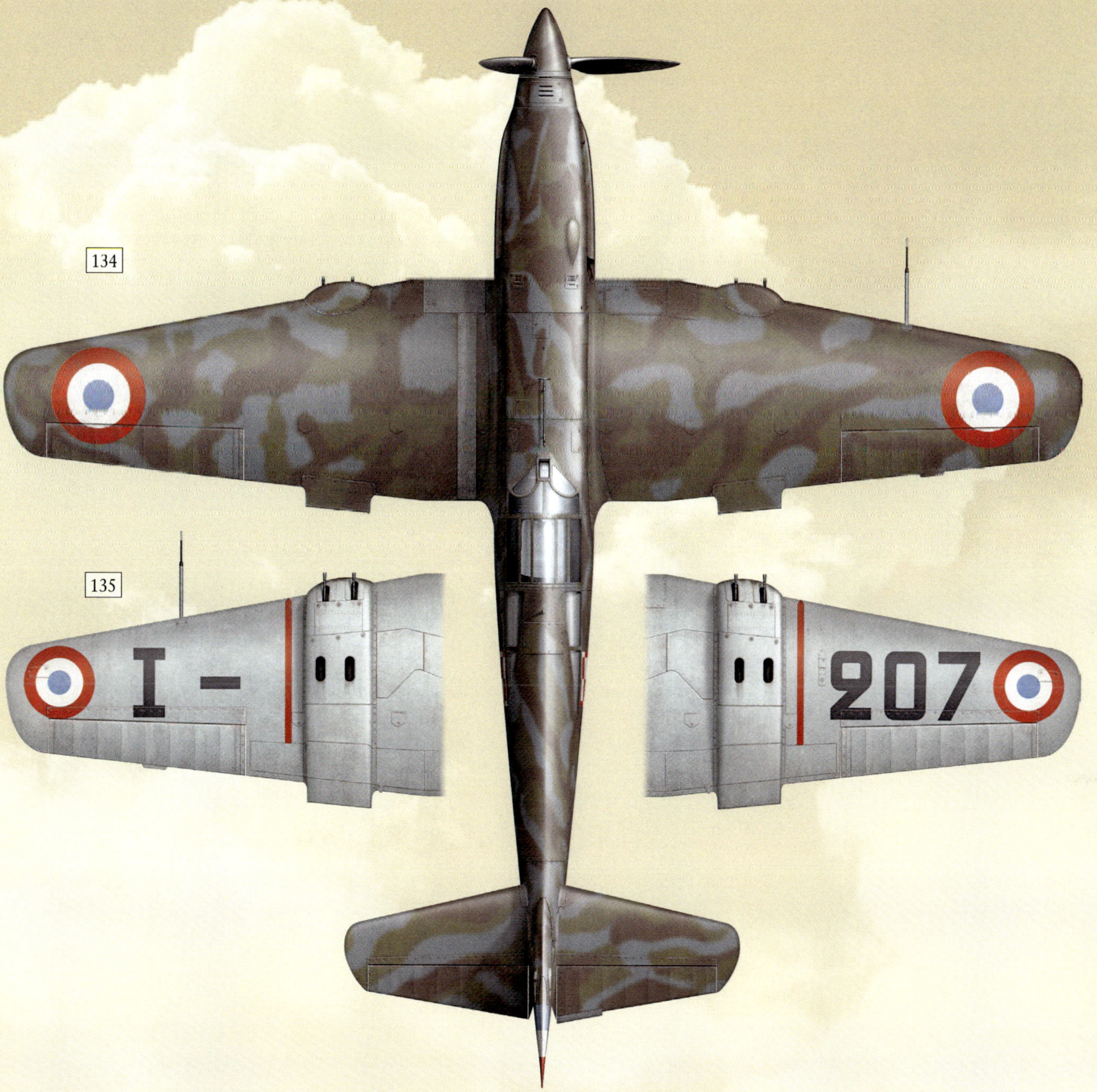

[136]: CR.714 c/n 8549 at Evreux, still with the Polish national marking on the fuselage. As time passed, it underwent gradual destruction. (G. Zaleski coll.)

136

[137, 139]: *Caudron-Renault CR.714 c/n 8550 (under-wing no. I-208), pilot – 2nd Lt Marian Łukaszewicz, 1 Esc. GC 1/145. Dreux, June 1940.*

137

138

[138]: The Caudron of 2nd Lt Łukaszewicz with the camouflage pattern on the port side shown to advantage. The last entry in Łukaszewicz's flying log book related to c/n 8550 mentioned that the aeroplane landed near the airfield with a stationary propeller. This may indicate a landing at Garennes-sur-Eure, about 15 km north of Dreux. Another possible location is around the Rue de la Garrenne in the northern suburbs of Dreux. (B. Belcarz coll.)

139

140

[140]: The aeroplane of 2nd Lt Marian Łukaszewicz from the 1 Esc GC 1/145 later on, as shown by progressing destruction. The Germans had captured it in almost perfect condition and it was only afterwards that it was vandalised. (M. Comas coll.)

[141]: Caudron-Renault CR.714 c/n 8556 (under-wing no. I-214), pilot – Cpl Edward Paterek, 2 Esc. GC 1/145. The aeroplane crash-landed at Chartres when flown by Maj. J. Kępiński, June 1940.

141

142

[142]: Kępiński's Caudron at the Chartres airfield. The damage to the fuselage just behind the cockpit confirms the serious wounds suffered by Kępiński. He was taken to a hospital at Chartres and was then evacuated to Vichy before the Germans arrived. The aeroplane was formally assigned to Cpl Paterek, but in its last sortie it was flown by the GC 1/145 commander Maj. Kępiński (his personal aeroplane had been seriously damaged on 9 June 1940). In his last sortie Kępiński was shot down, but he managed to reach the airfield at Chartres. This was the only Caudron at that airfield. The bent propeller blades testify to a belly landing. (B. Belcarz coll.)

[143]: *Caudron-Renault CR.714 c/n 85?? (under-wing no. I-2??), pilot – Lt Zbigniew Wróblewski, 2 Esc. GC 1/145, June 1940.*

143

144

[144]: The Caudron with code no. 16 on the fuselage was assigned to 2nd Lt Z. Wróblewski. The aeroplane made a wheels-up landing at a different location, not Dreux, but it has not been possible to identify the place where the photo was taken. (B. Belcarz coll.)

Główczyński, 2nd Lt Jerzy Czerniak, Cpl Andrzej Niewiara and LAC Ernest Watolski. It went to the GC I/8 that also flew Bloch 152s.

On 11 June the squadron was based at the Malesherbes–Césarville airfield. Sending the Poles to the GC I/1 and the GC I/8 was part of the plan of converting onto a new type of aircraft. The move to the GC I/8 made no significant difference for pilots because both units were based at the same airfield.[58] Formally, the departure of the group of Capt. Frey took place at Châteauroux on 16 June.[59] The plan of conversion training for the new type was supplemented by the decision to allocate three Bloch 152 aircraft from the GC I/8 to the GC 1/145. These were c/ns 149 (Y-636), 156 (Y-643) and 202 (Y-689) from the 2 Esc. of the GC I/8, which had a surplus of aircraft. The GC 1/145 pilots started their training on the new type rather unfortunately, damaging the undercarriage of c/n 149 at Césarville on 12 June.[60] Slightly damaged, this machine had to be abandoned. Eventually, eleven CR.714s and two Bloch MB 152s departed from Sermaises to Châteauroux. In the face of another evacuation, Col. Pawlikowski and Capt. Grzebalski went to Chartres on 13 June to evacuate Maj. Kępiński from the hospital. Once they arrived there, it turned out that the hospital had been moved to the south of France, but its exact location was not known.[61] So, they both returned to GC 1/145.

58 M. Comas, *Les chasseurs Caudron*, p. 60

59 *Capt*. Łaguna writes clearly (but incorrectly) in his report that "On 14 June 8 more pilots were to depart [to] 1/8, but this did not happen."

60 GC 1/145 Daily orders no. 25 p. 2 of 15 June 1940

61 Pilot unknown.

Châteauroux

14–17 June

The move of the GC 1/145 took place on the night of 13 June 1940. The air party flew in adverse weather conditions, while the ground party had to make its way through roads crowded with refugees.

At Châteauroux–La Martinerie the GC 1/145 was given the task of air defence of the town and the airfield. A total of seven combat missions were flown during 14-17 June in this role. Three sections were scrambled between 19.30 and 20.30 on 14 June. There were no encounters with the enemy, so the area around the airfield was patrolled at about 4,000–4,500 meters.

GC 1/145 aircraft took off three times on 15 June. Two sections between 8.05 and 9.30, and then one section between 10.15 and 10.55, patrolled own airfield area.

[145]: Burnt wreckage of Bloch MB 152 c/n 156 (Y-643) code no. 12 at the Rochefort airfield. It was ferried to the GC 1/145 from Brétigny by a Czech pilot, Sgt chef Prchal (Prchal was the pilot of the Liberator in which the Polish Commander-in-Chief General Władysław Sikorski was killed when it crashed at Gibraltar on 4 July 1943). (M. Comas coll.)

145

Cpl Jan Marciniak, a mechanic of the *1 Escadrille*, was taken to the hospital at Châteauroux on 15 June with a broken leg.

The same day, a group of Polish pilots from the GC I/55, led by Maj. Krasnodębski, were met.

The GC 1/145 remained at Châteauroux. On 16 June, the pilots took off twice in the strength of one section, but just like the previous day there was no contact with the enemy. Both operations were flown before midday (7.05–8.05 and 10.30–11.30).

Rochefort

17–18 June

The development of the situation at the front line forced another move of the squadron. On 17 June, the unit arrived at Rochefort, where it was given the task of air defence of the airfield.

In the last days of the combat operations, ground crew soldiers kept guard at the aeroplanes at the airfield, faced with the growing threat from the Germans. Col. Pawlikowski, who established contact with the French authorities, received conflicting orders from them regarding the tasks for the GC 1/145. In this situation, he tried to contact the Polish authorities, which he eventually managed to do.

On 17 and 18 June, on the orders of Col. Pawlikowski, the squadron was joined by the DAT sections of Maj. Krasnodębski (together with the sections of Lt Paszkiewicz and Lt Skiba) and Capt. Kowalczyk.

At Rochefort, all pilots of the GC 1/145 have come together again: also the pilots from the GC I/1 and the GC I/8 arrived at the airfield. This was not for long, because the GC I/1 moved to Royan-Médis, and the GC I/8 to Royan Corme-L'Écluse.

The GC 1/145 was at readiness from 9.00 on 19 June 1940, despite the fact that the French authorities had evacuated from La Rochelle the previous night. In that situation, preparations for evacuation were started.

Eleven CR.714s were left at Rochefort, seven of which were operationally serviceable. The following machines were identified as left at Rochefort: Capt. Łaguna's CR.714 '=' from the GC 1/145 HQ; *1 Escadrille* aircraft: code nos. 3, 7, 8; and *2 Escadrille* aircraft: 1, 2 and 11. Moreover, the GC 1/145 handed over two Bloch MB 152s (c/ns 156 and 202).

[146]: The part of the Rochefort airfield where aeroplanes were stored. On the right, two Bloch MB.151s can be seen, including c/n 23 in the foreground. On the left side, from the front towards the back: two Caudrons from the GC 1/145 (c/n 8584 (I-242) code no. 2 of 2nd Lt Czesław Główczyński is second left), a Morane Saulnier MS.406, a Koolhoven FK-58 (with a cover on the engine) and a Bloch MB.131 bomber. (Ph. Ricco coll.)

146

Evacuation La Rochelle – Perpignan

19 June

Organised evacuation began in that area on 19 June 1940 and took place earlier than the evacuation of other Polish aviation units. It was forced by the situation at the front line and by the threat from German troops that occupied Nantes that day, about 150 km north of Rochefort. The Polish fighter squadron, GC 1/145, was still in the Rochefort area, and continued to provide air defence until the end. It did not leave the airfield until about 9.00 on 19 June, moving to the port of La Rochelle. The Poles' departure took place after the evacuation of the French troops, who had left the Rochefort airfield on the night of 18 June 1940. Eleven Caudron-Renault CR.714s and two Bloch MB 152s were left at the airfield.

Upon arrival at La Rochelle, the Polish transport was loaded on a French ship about midday, to be evacuated. However, two hours later there was a change of orders and the airmen had to disembark. In that situation Col. Pawlikowski asked assistance from the British consulate, where he was assured that the Polish unit would be embarked the same day onto a British ship. Indeed, three British vessels wharfed about 18.00 and started embarkation, which was completed the next morning, whence they sailed to the Britain escorted by two destroyers. The Poles found themselves on board SS 'Alderpool', a 3,000 GRT ship.

Six pilots of the squadron were missing from the evacuation list: Wilczewski, Zadroziński, Czerniak, Jaugsch, Watolski and Niewiara.

Probably in the heat of evacuation they failed to reach the squadron. This hypothesis is confirmed by the registration data of Polish officers and NCOs in Britain. These reported their arrival in England on 12 July (Wilczewski, Jaugsch), 16 (Zadroziński, Czerniak and Watolski) and 17 July 1940 (Niewiara). Pilots of the GC 1/145 who sailed from La Rochelle were registered in Britain on 21 June 1940. The July arrival dates for six of them indicate that they must have been evacuated from the Mediterranean ports of France (Port Vendres?) to Africa, and then through Gibraltar to Britain.

The list of GC 1/145 pilots evacuated from France was as follows:

La Rochelle (La Pallice)	Perpignan	Port Vendres
Capt. Piotr Łaguna Lt Julian Kowalski Lt Tadeusz Czerwiński 2nd Lt Marian Łukasiewicz 2nd Lt Eugeniusz Fiedorczuk 2nd Lt Zbigniew Wróblewski Cpl Władysław Uher Capt. Juliusz Frey 2nd Lt Czesław Główczyński Lt Marian Szalewicz 2nd Lt Bolesław Gładych Sergt. Edward Paterek Sergt. Jan Palak LAC Jerzy Zieliński Col. Stefan Pawlikowski	Capt. Antoni Wczelik 2nd Lt Bronisław Skibiński 2nd Lt Aleksy Żukowski Sergt. Antoni Markiewicz Sergt. Lucjan Szempliński Cpl Mieczysław Parafiński Cpl Piotr Zaniewski LAC Antoni Joda	Lt Jerzy Godlewski Capt. Franciszek Fugiel

147

[147]: The photograph of 2nd Lt Fiedorczuk's code no. 8 is one of the best known images. However, although there are several known photos of this aircraft now, its construction and serial numbers remain unknown. (R. Gretzyngier coll.)

[148]: Caudron-Renault CR.714 c/n 8586 (under-wing no. I-244), pilot – 2nd Lt Marian Szalewicz, 2 Esc. GC 1/145. Rochefort, June 1940.

148

149

[149]: The c/n 8586 of this aircraft was identified by deciphering the under-wing Matricule Militaire. The aeroplane belonged to the 2 Escadrille and was flown by 2nd Lt Marian Szalewicz, with code no. 4 on the fuselage. (B. Belcarz coll.)

150

151

[150–153]: Caudron-Renault CR.714 c/n 8584 (under-wing no. I-242) pilot – 2nd Lt Czesław Główczyński, 2 Esc. GC 1/145. Rochefort, June 1940.

152

153

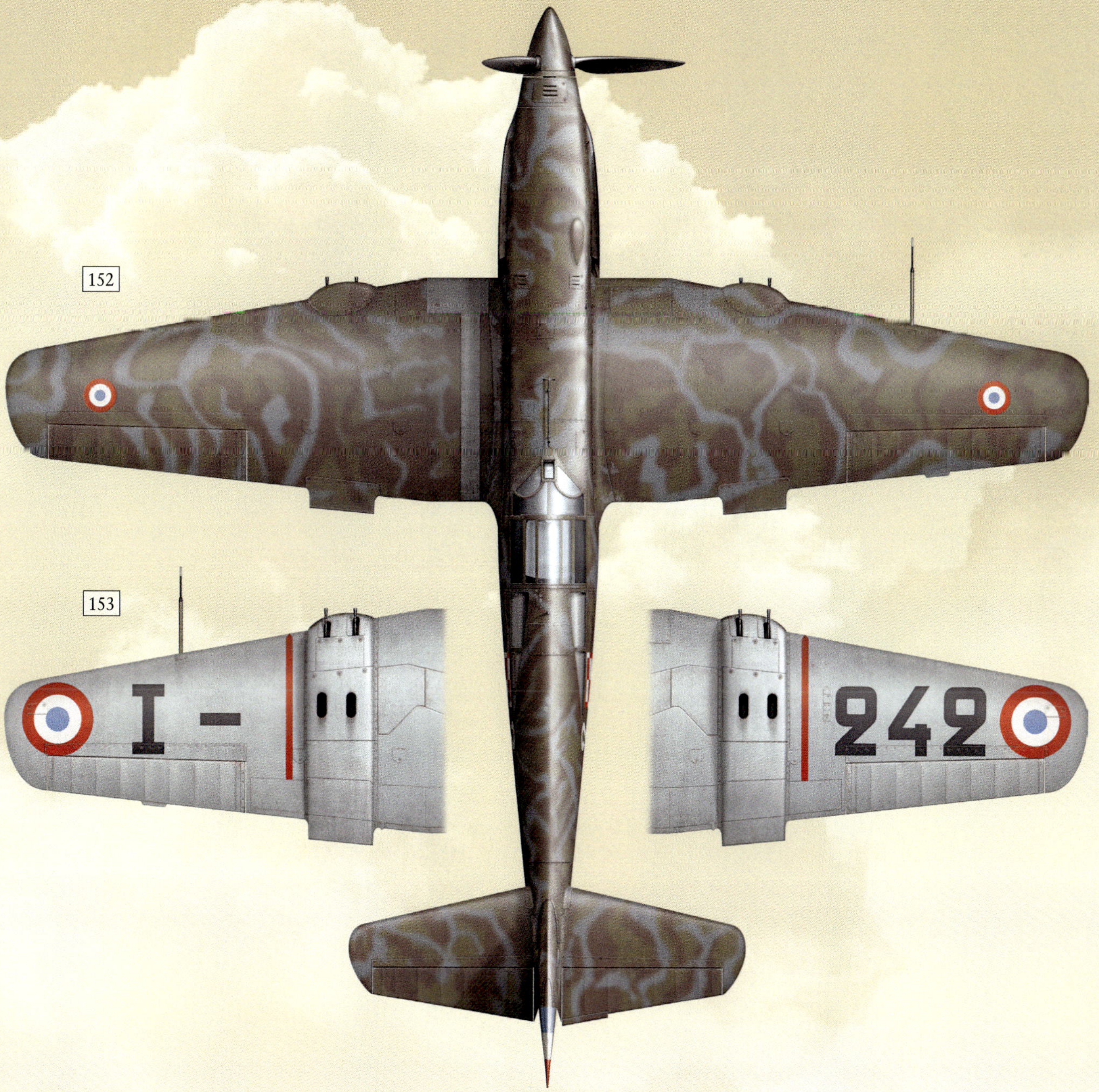

154

[154]: CR.714 c/n 8584 (I-242), code no. 2, of 2nd Lt Czesław Główczyński from the 2 Esc. The photo shows clearly the standard set of data applied on the fin and rudder. The absence of the military serial number and of the weight/loading figures is noteworthy (compare fig. [189] on p. 102). (B. Belcarz coll.)

155

[155, 156]: *These photographs have been among the oldest known images of GC 1/145 Caudrons, but escaped identification because the white code number 2 on the fuselage could not be seen. Only after other pictures of no. 2 were found, comparison of the camouflage pattern allowed identification of the aeroplane as the machine of 2nd Lt Główczyński. Note the clearly visible late-style undercarriage and the absence of large upper undercarriage covers on both sides. (B. Belcarz coll.)*

156

157

[157, 158]: The GC 1/145 staff left their aeroplanes dispersed on the entire surface of the Rochefort airfield, according to the principles of passive anti-aircraft defence. This is documented by these photos of the aeroplane of 2nd Lt Główczyński.

158

[159]: Caudron-Renault CR.714 c/n 8554 (under-wing no. I-212), pilot – Capt. Piotr Łaguna, GC 1/145 HQ. Rochefort, June 1940.

159

160

[160]: Capt. Piotr Łaguna took over the duties of the squadron commander after the heavily wounded Maj. Kępiński was hospitalised at Chartres on 10 June 1940. Łaguna commanded the unit during the withdrawal, until the final evacuation from France. C/n 8554 (I-212) was his personal machine and it remained with the unit until the very end. The aircraft bore no code number but, similar to the aeroplane of Maj. Kępiński, it featured a simple geometric marking. Two white horizontal stripes of the deputy commander were applied on the fin. The aeroplane was finally captured by the Germans at Rochefort. The port lower engine cowling had very characteristic area of peeling paint, which is a giveaway of this machine. (B. Belcarz coll.)

[161]: Caudron-Renault CR.714 c/n 85??, pilot – Capt. Juliusz Frey, 2 Esc. GC 1/145. Rochefort, June 1940.

[162]: CR.714 code no. 1 from the 2 Esc., captured by the Germans in very good condition. Unfortunately, its serial or construction number could not be ascertained. At least two other, unidentified aircraft of the type can be seen in the background. (B. Belcarz coll.)

[163, 165]: *Caudron-Renault CR.714 no 85??, pilot – 2nd Lt Leon Jaugsch, 2 Esc. GC 1/145. Rochefort, June 1940.*

[164]: The CR.714 code no. 11 of 2nd Lt Leon Jaugsch from the 2 Esc. with other aircraft. On the left: the nose of code no. 8 and code no. 3, c/n 8575 (I-233), both of the 1 Esc. The one behind no. 11 is CR.714 c/n 8554 (I-212) of Capt. Piotr Łaguna, the last commander of the GC /145. (B. Belcarz coll.)

[165]: Caudron-Renault CR.714 c/n 85??, pilot – Lt Tadeusz Czerwiński, 1 Esc. GC 1/145. Rochefort, June 1940.

165

166

[166]: Lt Tadeusz Czerwiński's CR.714 code no. 7 from the 1 Esc. of the GC 1/145 at Rochefort. Note the canvas cover on the propeller spinner and blades. The aeroplane featured the early undercarriage type, differing in this respect from CR.714 code no. 2 from the 2 Esc., with which it had been confused in older publications. (B. Belcarz coll.)

[167]: Caudron-Renault CR.714 no 8575, (under-wing no. I-233) pilot – Capt. Antoni Wczelik, 1 Esc. GC 1/145. Rochefort, June 1940.

167

168

[168]: CR.714 c/n 8575 (I-233) of Capt. Antoni Wczelik, the 1 Esc. commander, which displayed code no. 3 on the fin. Note the tail of 2nd Lt Fiedorczuk's CR.714 code no. 8 on the left. (B. Belcarz coll.)

[169, 171]: *Caudron-Renault CR.714 c/n 85??, pilot – 2nd Lt Eugeniusz Fiedorczuk, 1 Esc. GC 1/145. Rochefort, June 1940.*

169

170

[170]: This photo of 2nd Lt Fiedorczuk's CR.714 code no. 8 shows the camouflage pattern on the port side of the fuselage. Unfortunately, it does not reveal the aircraft's serial or construction number. (G. Zaleski coll.)

171

Camouflage & markings

The camouflage and markings of the Caudron CR.714 was in accordance with the relevant standards in force between 1938 and 1940. Some deviations resulted only from problems with the production start-up, its slow rate, and changing opinions of the ordering party as to the future use of the aircraft.

Camouflage

The contract (no. 1646/8) for the production and delivery of Caudron CR.714s was signed on 2 December 1938. In accordance with the standard in force at the time, the aircraft leaving factories were supposed to be finished in *kaki* (khaki) on upper surfaces and *gris bleu clair* (pale blue grey) on under surfaces. Contracts signed during peace time were not annexed or modified with respect to the painting scheme on production aircraft. An aircraft left the factory in a scheme that complied with the original contract specification. Corrections of the scheme to match current requirements, where these had changed, were applied after acceptance. Therefore, until the production run ended in June 1940, the CR.714s were leaving the assembly line in the uniform scheme. That was the appearance of the more or less complete aircraft captured by the Germans at the factory airfield at Guyancourt and of a few late production machines that could be taken on charge by the Armée de l'Air before the armistice. The khaki hue in the scheme is shown in various ways in black and white photos, ranging from a relatively pale to very dark, depending on the photographic material and on the lighting of the glossy surfaces of the aircraft. This suggests application of the glossy khaki paint with a dark green or olive green hue (*vert kaki foncé*), commonly used before 1939.[1] Thus the production of Caudron CR.714s was not affected with the instruction dated 6 December 1939, which ordered manufacturers to apply a camouflage scheme that consisted of khaki (*kaki*), *brun* (brown) and *gris bleu foncé* (dark grey blue) on upper surfaces. The first production CR.714, no. 1 (c/n 8533, MM I-191), completed and flown in June 1939, is the only known factory fresh machine from 1939 that featured such multi-tone camouflage. It is commonly known from several catalogue-type photos. Its camouflage pattern is very clear and regular, and it resembles nothing of what can be seen on later machines.[2] Six more CR.714s were built during the summer of 1939 (the ones that were delivered to Finland in late April 1940), but they were then grounded, with over a dozen subsequent machines, virtually until the end of 1939, due to a wing design error that was detected.[3] Because the contract could not be completed on time, and because the performance

1 During research and restoration work on Caudron CR.714 no. 8538, a coat of dark green or olive green paint (approx. FS 14052–14064) was discovered beneath the camouflage (at least on metal components of the fuselage). It had been applied as an intermediate layer between the transparent primer and the actual camouflage. This was clearly similar to the older variants of *kaki*.

2 The same machine in its subsequent form, while used by the 1st Flight of the GC 1/145 (white 14) in June 1940, had a completely altered camouflage pattern and markings, and had had its undercarriage replaced with the late type (Messier).

3 The date on the inspection plate on the wing of CR 714 no. 6 (c/n 8538) is '12-1939'.

[172]: The bottom of the rear fuselage of the Caudron CR.714. Despite substantial damage to the paint finish, the division line between the upper surface camouflage and the under surface colour can be seen clearly. Note that the colour division did not follow the metal panel edge. The same applies to almost all known fully camouflaged examples. The yellowish patches are traces of an organic, transparent primer. Utti, 29 April 2015. (B. Belcarz)

The official name of the color	English name	Federal Standard
Kaki (Vert Foncé) brillant	Khaki (Dark Green) gloss	FS 14052* - FS 14064*
Kaki mat	Khaki	FS 33070* – FS34127*
Brun mat	Dark Brown	FS 20062*
Gris Bleu Foncé mat	Dark Blue Grey	FS 36099* – FS 36173*
Gris Bleu Clair mat	Light Blue Grey	FS 35237*

* *approximate*

Kaki (Vert Foncé) brilliant

Kaki mat

Brun mat

Gris Bleu Foncé mat

Gris Bleu Clair mat

was inadequate, the Armée de l'Air was losing interest in the aircraft. Although the contract was not cancelled, the Caudron 714 became, in a way, an unassigned type, intended for exports or for training only. It is therefore easy to guess that updating its camouflage or markings were no longer priorities. It seems most likely that the multi-tone camouflage did not appear on the Caudrons until late 1939 or early 1940, when the rate of production and deliveries of these machines increased. The multi-tone camouflage was applied to finished aircraft, possibly outside the parent factory, but using paints with hues as recommended for the industry. In any case, such hues could be seen on the surviving CR.714 no. 6 (c/n 8538) and on the remains of no. 5 (c/n 8537). We can assume that the colours: *kaki*, *brun*, *gris bleu foncé* and *gris bleu clair* were worn by most if not all CR.714s used by Polish flyers. The greyscale tones of the camouflage in most black and white photos of the CR.714s do not differ from those in photos of other types of series-produced French aircraft.

The pattern and style of camouflage areas on the CR.714s were much varied. It seems that there was no prescribed pattern, not even a very general one, for the type. It is worth noting that no large regular areas or broad bands of individual colours could be seen. The colour areas on the CR.714 were irregular, rather small, and were cloud-shaped or formed in narrow streaks that followed various shapes. The camouflage style on a single machine was usually constant, and the colour division lines were soft. The position of the division line between the upper camouflage and the bottom colour, located below the panel lines of the engine cowling or the fuselage, was a common feature. In violation of the standard in force, which called for the propeller spinners to be painted black, all CR.714s had their spinners in camouflage colours. Paints used to apply the camouflage gave smooth matt surface finish.

National markings

Rudder bands

The three-tone vertical bands of equal width that covered the entire rudder surface were a standard marking. They were applied with glossy paints in the following colours (front to aft): blue (*bleu cocarde*), white (*blanc*), and red (*rouge cocarde*).

National markings on the wings

The national markings (roundels) on the wings were in the form of concentric blue, white and red circles with a diameter ratio of 1: 2: 3, applied with the same paints as the rudder bands. The under-wing roundels had a diameter of 0.60 m. Aircraft no. 1 (c/n 8533) in its initial form of 1939 featured approx. 0.80 m under-wing roundels. 0.30 m roundels were applied on upper wing surfaces of the CR.714s, in accordance with the standard of December 1938. Although this size became officially obsolete as of autumn 1939, such small markings were applied at the factory until the end of the CR.714 production run in June 1940. A part of the CR.714s had larger, 0.80 m, roundels on the upper wing surfaces. Such roundels were applied outside the factory, probably following the camouflage modification. Such large roundels could be seen on some Caudrons of the GC 1/145, but all known machines from the CWL/DIAP Lyon still had the small roundels.

[173]: Caudron-Renault CR.714 c/n 8593 (under-wing no. I-251). Bordeaux, June 1940.

173

174

[174]: CR.714 c/n 8593 (I-251) at Bordeaux in late June 1940. Although this particular aircraft had no known Polish connection, it provides a good illustration of the appearance of CR.714s as they left the Caudron assembly line at Guyancourt. The aeroplane is finished in a single-tone glossy dark khaki scheme on upper surfaces and pale blue grey underneath. (G. Zaleski coll.)

[175]: Examples of two different sizes of French national markings on the CR.714 wing upper surface. The small, 0.30 m markings were applied at the factory until the end of CR.714 production, in accordance with the instruction of 7 December 1938. The large, ca. 0.80 m ones were applied after delivery and followed the regulations of 19 November 1939. They could be seen on some aircraft of the GC 1/145, but there is no known connection between their presence and the construction/ serial numbers.

175

National markings on the fuselage

The fuselage roundels on the CR.714s, similar to most other types, started to be applied at the factory probably at the beginning of 1940. They were applied in a standard position, below the rear cockpit glazing. Their diameter, 0.42 m, matched the design of the CR.714. No deviations from this rule are known.

176

Caudrons used by Polish flyers had the fuselage roundel overpainted with the Polish national marking in the form of a 0.42 x 0.42 m white and red square. Similar to other aircraft types at the DIAP Lyon (mostly MS.406s), the roundel was showing through the Polish markings. This could not be seen on the Caudrons used by the GC 1/145. Evidently, the Polish markings were applied more carefully here, but there seems no doubt that these aircraft had had the French markings on the fuselage.

[176]: Location of French roundels and the under-wing number (Matricule Militaire) on the lower surface of the wings. All known CR.714s flown by the Poles featured the 0.60 m roundels on wing under surfaces.

177

[177]: Application of the Polish national markings on French aeroplanes showed some variations. The Polish square-shaped markings were applied on top of the French roundels. Various transparency effects were seen, depending on the quality of the paint used. In general, the overpainted original markings showed through quite prominently on the aircraft of the DIAP Lyon (MS.406s and one known CR.714, no. I-204). Later on, the aeroplanes delivered to the GC 1/145 had the Polish markings applied more carefully, so that the French ones did not show through.

[178]: The code numbers were applied on the fin at the DIAP at Lyon-Bron. At least seven CR.714s were marked this way. Existing photographs make it possible to reconstruct the appearance of four of these. The Lyon code numbers were the largest of all those applied on CR.714s. The height of the code number on Lyon-Bron aircraft was approximately 0.60 m.

178

[179]: Eleven aircraft from the 1 Esc., ten from the 2 Esc., and two from the HQ section have been identified in surviving photographs. The appearance of known GC 1/145 CR.714 code numbers is shown below to the same scale, for comparison of their respective size. 1 Escadrille aircraft numbers were 0.32 m high. Code no. 14 was an exception, its height clearly smaller, ca. 26–27 cm.

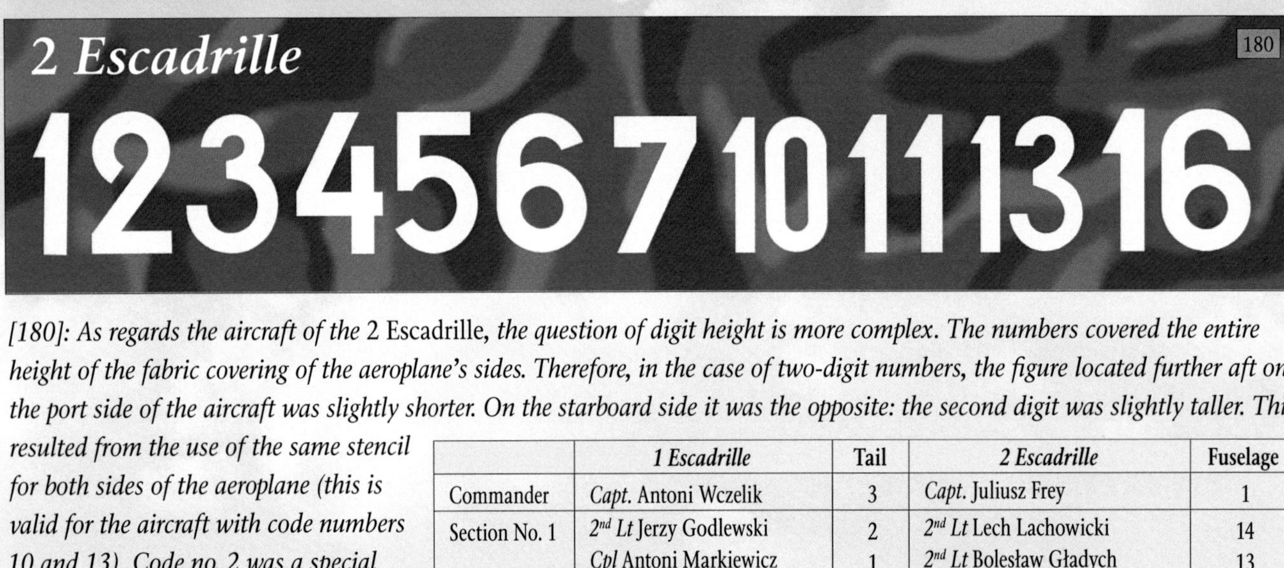

[180]: As regards the aircraft of the 2 Escadrille, *the question of digit height is more complex. The numbers covered the entire height of the fabric covering of the aeroplane's sides. Therefore, in the case of two-digit numbers, the figure located further aft on the port side of the aircraft was slightly shorter. On the starboard side it was the opposite: the second digit was slightly taller. This resulted from the use of the same stencil for both sides of the aeroplane (this is valid for the aircraft with code numbers 10 and 13). Code no. 2 was a special case: it was applied in a somewhat crooked form, with the horizontal bar matching the bottom edge of the covering. Thus it is hard to quote a uniform height for it. It did not exceed 0.40 m and was presumably not less than 0.38 m. The dimensions have been determined by comparing photos and known dimensions of the aircraft in the relevant places.*

	1 Escadrille	Tail	*2 Escadrille*	Fuselage
Commander	*Capt.* Antoni Wczelik	3	*Capt.* Juliusz Frey	1
Section No. 1	2nd *Lt* Jerzy Godlewski	2	2nd *Lt* Lech Lachowicki	14
	Cpl Antoni Markiewicz	1	2nd *Lt* Bolesław Gładych	13
	Vacancy	-	*LAC* Andrzej Niewiara	10
Section No. 2	*Lt* Jan Obuchowski	4	*Lt* Wacław Wilczewski	9
	2nd Lt Bronisław Skibiński	5	2nd *Lt* Leon Jaugsch	11
	LAC Mieczysław Parafiński	6	*Cpl* Edward Paterek	5
Section No. 3	*Lt* Tadeusz Czerwiński	7	*Lt* Zdzisław Zadroziński	7
	2nd *Lt* Eugeniusz Fiedorczuk	8	*Cpl* Jan Palak	12
	Cpl Ladislav Uher	9	*LAC* Edward Uchto	8
Section No. 4	*Lt* Julian Kowalski	10	2nd *Lt* Czesław Główczyński	2
	2nd *Lt* Marian Łukaszewicz	11	2nd *Lt* Jerzy Czerniak	6
	Cpl Lucjan Szempliński	12	*LAC* Ernest Watolski	3
Section No. 5	2nd *Lt* Aleksy Żukowski	13	2nd *Lt* Marian Szalewicz	4
	LAC Antoni Joda	14	2nd *Lt* Zbigniew Wróblewski	16
	LAC Piotr Zaniewski	15	*LAC* Jerzy Zieliński	15

Matricule Militaire (MM) numbers

The Matricule Militaire (MM) number was applied on wing under surfaces, which consisted of a letter and three digits. This was a military equivalent of the civil registration and allowed identification of the aircraft from the ground. On early machines the number was also applied on the rear fuselage. The fuselage MM numbers could be seen on aircraft of the DIAP Lyon, but not on those of the GC 1/145.

The MM number on the CR.714 consisted of the letter 'I' and a dash applied on the bottom of the starboard wing, and three digits on the bottom of the port wing. As an example, the first machine (military serial no. 1, c/n 8533) had the MM number I-191. The MM numbers of subsequent aircraft were sequential, synchronised with the serial number.

181

[181, 182]: The Matricule Militaire *number I-205 on the fuselage, approx. 0.24 m tall. The Polish marking was 0.42 m across (similar to other machines), its rear lower corner usually overlapping the bottom metal fuselage panel.*

182

Although the MM numbers ceased to be applied on newly built aircraft of other types at the beginning of 1940, they continued to be painted on the CR.714s until the end of the production run.

The MM number characters on the wings were approx. 0.60 m high and had a special style, as shown in the plate. The fuselage number, if applied, was approx. 0.24 m high.

Manufacturer, type and serial number designations

Each CR.714 had a four-digit construction number (such as 8533) applied at the top of the fin. It was panted by hand in black and was approx. 30 mm high. The name of the maker, CAUDRON-RENAULT, and an italicised type name in quotation marks, *"Cyclone"*, were also applied on the fin.

In accordance with the regulations in force, the aircraft type name (CR.714C1) and the military serial number (such as N°1), were applied on the rudder. Weight and loading symbols (PT, PC, PE, ESSENCE, HUILE) were applied at the bottom of the rudder. The relevant numerical values were only added for the fuel (ESSENCE – 200) and oil (HUILE – 14). Application of the military serial number was discontinued at some point, the latest aircraft known to have this number applied was no. 27 (c/n 8559). All rudder markings were applied in black.

All principal assemblies of the aircraft were marked with its military serial number. These numbers were painted by hand in red. With exception of the number at the top of the rear frame in the cockpit and those in the mainwheel wells, they were not visible from the outside once the aircraft was assembled. The only known maintenance marking consisted of red stripes, approx. 60 mm wide, applied on wing under surfaces, outboard of the armament pods. These identified the position of the reinforced structure where the wings were to be trestled during assembly or maintenance. In accordance with the standards in force, the antenna tips were supposed to be finished in red.

Code numbers

Aircraft of the CWL/DIAP Lyon were marked with large white digits applied on the fin. At least seven machines featured these codes. The appearance of four of these can be reconstructed from photos: 1, 2, 3 and 6. The digits were approx. 0.60 m high.

Aircraft of the two flights of the GC 1/145 were also identified within the squadron by their code numbers.

Those of the GC 1/145's 1st Flight had code numbers between 1 and 15 applied on the fin, while those of the 2nd Flight had their code numbers, 1 to 16, applied on the fuselage.

The numbers applied on the fin were approx. 0.30 m high. The numbers on the fuselage were bigger, approx. 0.38–0.40 m high, matching the fabric-covering on the sides of the fuselage. In both cases there was no pre-defined style for the digits (see the plate).

Commanders' markings

Aircraft of the HQ section did not have code numbers, this being different from the standard practice in the French Air Force. Very simple markings were adopted on commanders'

183

184

[183–184]: Markings of the Polish GC 1/145 commanders were unusual when compared with those of their counterparts in the French Air Force. The aeroplane of Maj. Kępiński, c/n 8565 (I-223), featured a single horizontal thin stripe on both sides of the fin just below the construction number ([183]). The aeroplane of Capt. Łaguna, c/n 8554 (I-212), had two such stripes ([184]). During the campaign, the GC 1/145 was joined by Cdt de Marmier, who was assigned the aeroplane c/n 8589 (I-247). That aircraft had previously been assigned to Cpl Szempliński from the 1 Esc. and marked with code no. 12. Surviving photos show no additional marking on this machine.

185

186

[185]: Metal identification plate with the c/n (8538), the aeroplane type designation (714) and the date (12-1939). (M. Kolunen)

[186]: Construction number 8538 applied on the fin of the Finnish CR.714.

187

N°8559

[187]: Construction number, approx. 30 mm high.

188

N° 27

[188]: The military serial number.

White code number applied at the DIAP Lyon on the fin only.

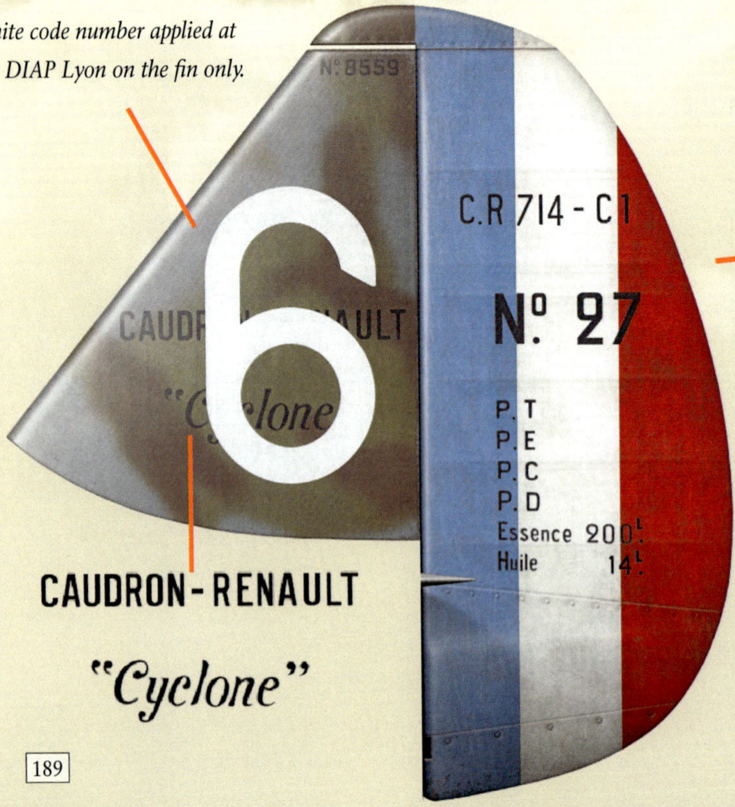

189

PT = Poids totale – *total weight, (PE+PC+PD)*
PE = Poids Équipé – *empty weight (airframe + engine)*
PC = Poids Carburant – *fuel weight (petrol + oil) sometimes broken down into:*
E = Essence *(petrol)*
H = Huile *(oil)*
or PC= E + H
PD (or P) = Poids Divers miscellaneous weights (in practice: crew + ammunition)

aircraft in the GC 1/145: a single white horizontal stripe at the top of the fin for the unit commander, Maj. Kępiński, and two horizontal stripes for his deputy, Capt. Łaguna.

No unit or personal emblems are known to have been applied on the CR.714s. Similarly, no code markings are known to have been applied on the few machines used by French pilots.

Colours of the interior and other details

The cockpit interior was finished in medium blue-grey (FS 36152 is an almost ideal equivalent). The cockpit floor was of varnished plywood. The instrument panel was black. Radio equipment components were painted steely grey.

The interior of the metal sections of the fuselage, armament pods, wing flaps, undercarriage covers, and the mainwheel wells were finished with the blue-grey paint, the same hue as the cockpit interior. The inside wing surface above the landing flaps, visible through the lightening holes, was of varnished plywood.

Mainwheel legs and hubs, supplied by subcontractors, were painted glossy blue-grey, slightly paler than the interior but darker than the aircraft under surfaces. The oil tank in the port wing leading edge near the fuselage and the walkway on the port wing were left in natural metal finish. Propeller blades were painted matt black on both sides. At least several CR.714s of the DIAP Lyon featured the double pale stripes on propeller blade tips, also known from the MS.406s of the unit.

Visible technical differences

Some Caudrons, mainly the early ones, did not have the balance tab on the rudder. This applies to all machines sent to Finland and to aircraft of the CWL/DIAP Lyon. The balance tab is present on all other known machines, including all those of the GC 1/145.

The CR.714 aircraft were fitted with two undercarriage variants, known commonly as 'early' (A.M.C.D.) and 'late' (Messier). There is no precise or consequent connection of these with the serial numbers. Known aircraft with the 'late' undercarriage are nos. 1 (8533) in its June 1940 form, 9 (8541), 43 (8575), 52 (8584), 56 (8587), 58 (8589), 59 (8591), and 62 (8594), and most of the unfinished ones captured by the Germans at the Guyancourt factory.

190

[190]: CR.714 from the DIAP Lyon, serial/code number unknown. This aeroplane and two other, also with unknown numbers, provided backdrop for the ceremony on 27 March 1940. The twin pale stripes on the propeller blades are shown clearly. These were also seen on MS.406s from the same establishment. (MLP)

[191–192]: Two photos showing undercarriage variants in production CR.714s. Photo [191] shows the 'early' (A.M.C.D.) design, [192] shows the 'late' (Messier) one. (Keski-Suomen Ilmailumuseo/Finnish Air Force Museum, B. Belcarz)

191

192

[193–195]: Details of the finish of Caudron CR.714 c/n 8538, brought from Finland to the Polish Aviation Museum in Cracow in 2015 as a long term deposit. Careful cleaning of the aeroplane revealed the original 1940 colours. (J. Dobrzyński)

193

194

195